The Origin and Principles of the American Revolution Compared

With the Origin and Principles of the
French Revolution

By

Friedrich Gentz

*Translated with Preface by
John Quincy Adams*

Introduction by
Stephen A. Flick, PhD

Christian Heritage Press

The Origin and Principles of the American Revolution Compared

With the Origin and Principles of the French Revolution

By *Friedrich Gentz*

Translated with Preface by
John Quincy Adams

©2019 Stephen A. Flick

All rights reserved. No part of this publication may be reproduced, stored in a retrieval system or transmitted in any form or by any means, electronic, mechanical, photocopying, recording or otherwise without the prior permission of the publisher or in accordance with the provisions of the Copyright, Designs and Patents Act 1988 or under the terms of any license permitting limited copying issued by the Copyright Licensing Agency.

Published by:
Christian Heritage Fellowship, Inc.
1121 N. Charles G. Seivers Blvd, #143
Clinton, TN 37717

Cover Design: Stephen A. Flick

ISBN-13: 9798647670106

Printed in USA

DEDICATION

To dear friends, Tammy and Keith, whose friendship has
brightened my life's darkest days and whose
encouragement has emboldened the
voice of truth for America's
Christian heritage.

Contents

IMAGE CREDITS 6

WHY THIS IS IMPORTANT 9
Influence of Ministers and the Bible 10
About the Author and Translator 12
A Note Concerning Thomas Paine 15
Political vs Religious Observations 18
About This Edition 20

PREFACE 21

ORIGIN AND PRINCIPLES 23

REFERENCE NOTES 87

Image Credits

Arranged Alphabetically

Cover: Image Credits style — Man reads Declaration of Independence, by ReenactmentStock, Adobe Stock, Copyright.

Seedtime of the Republic, by unknown, Open Source, Public Domain.

Friedrich von Gentz, by Hans Wahl, Wikimedia Commons, Public Domain.

John Quincy Adams, by George Peter Alexander Healy, Wikimedia Commons, Public Domain.

Elias Boudinot, by Charles Willson Peale, Wikimedia Commons, Public Domain.

John Adams, by Asher B. Durand, Wikimedia Commons, Public Domain.

AMERICAN VS FRENCH REVOLUTION

Why This Is Important

By Stephen A. Flick

If the Gospel of Jesus Christ is to enjoy greater influence in America, the erroneous notion that America was conceived and founded by the irreligious must be soundly refuted. A populace that believes the lie that, "America was founded by Deists," will be deceptively convinced to reject the claims of Christianity upon their personal and collective lives. One of the many tools used to deceive Americans has been the suggestion that the principles that gave rise to the godless French Revolution were comparable to the influences that motivated America's Founding Fathers.

The ill-informed often suggest the American Revolution was comparable in its character and intent to the godless French Revolution of 1789. But, such a notion is historical fiction! Sadly, many Christians have bought into similar notions that the two Revolutions were parallel in their intent to free all people from oppression. In fact, many Christians have accepted the deceptive opinion that America's Founding Fathers were Deists, and, therefore, anti-Christian. Again, nothing could be further from historical reality. Yet, many so-called "Christian" authorities have produced books, videos, and other resources that sadly continue to perpetuate this lie.

INFLUENCE OF MINISTERS AND THE BIBLE

The principles that evoked the American Revolution arose out of convictions primarily strewn from the pulpits of Her churches. Prior to the late-nineteenth century—or before the rise of Darwinism—America's churches were pastored by ministers who believed the Bible. It is no surprise to recount the fact that religious freedom of Christians was a designing force in the origin of the Thirteen English Colonies in the New World.

Scholarship demonstrates that preachers were leading voices in the cause of American independence. In his book, *Seedtime of the Republic*, Clinton Rossiter[1] suggests there were six leading voices that shaped the thinking of Americans and motivated them toward freedom. Among the six, were two laymen, Richard Bland of Virginia and the venerable Benjamin Franklin of Philadelphia, Pennsylvania. The four remaining voices that influenced the principles of the American Revolution were all ministers of the Gospel and included Thomas Hooker (founder of Connecticut), Roger William (founder of Rhode Island), John Wise (pastor of the Chebacco Parish, Ipswich, Massachusetts), and Jonathan Mayhew (minister at Old West Church, Boston, Massachusetts).

The research of two scholars proves the formative influence accorded to the Bible by the Founding Fathers in general. Charles Hyneman was a Distinguished Professor of political science at Indiana University. Together with Donald S. Lutz, Associate Professor of Political Science at the University of Huston, these two professors reviewed an estimated 15,000 political documents from the founding era of America as an independent nation—an era of nearly half a century, extending from 1760 to 1805. Hyneman and Lutz published their findings in the early 1980s, and the results of their ten-year study were not kind to the fallacies of secularists. They showed that the single most often quoted source in the political writings of America's Founding Fathers was the Bible, receiving 34% of the total number of quotes. Donald Lutz summarized their work in his book, *The Origins of American Constitutionalism*, calling attention to the priority given to the Bible by the Founding Fathers:

> The relative influence of European thinkers on American political thought is a large and complex question not to be answered in any but a provisional way here. We can, however, identify the broad trends of influence and which European thinkers need to be especially considered. One means to this end is an examination of the citations in public political literature written between 1760 and 1805. If we ask which book was most frequently cited in that literature, the answer is, the Bible.[2]

Quotations from additional sources did not receive near the attention accorded to the Bible by the Fathers. Baron Charles Montesquieu ranked a distant second with 8.3% of the total quotes, followed by British legal scholar, William Blackstone, at 7.9%, and theologian and political writer, John Locke, was quoted 2.9% of the time in the quotes identified by Hyneman and Lutz.[3] Further, it should be noted that most of the individuals the Founding Fathers quoted in the Hyneman-Lutz study were Christian thinkers and authors. For years, secularists have insisted that irreligious Enlightenment thinkers were the primary source of influence upon the Founding Fathers, but in fact, the radical Enlightenment thinkers had very little impact upon the development of American political life.

One of the subsequent articles developed by Professor Lutz explained that the "First Enlightenment" thinkers were Christian and were credited with 16% of the political citations. The radical thinkers of the "Second Enlightenment," such as Voltaire, Diderot, and Helvetius, garnered only 2% of the citations while members of the "Third Enlightenment" era, typified by Rousseau, Mably, Raynal, and others, received a mere 4% of interest in the citations of the Founding Fathers.[4]

This study by two political science scholars clearly demonstrates dependence upon the Bible for some of the most "innovative" principles that eventually made their way into the United States Constitution. And, what was the source of inspiration for these "innovations"? As was noted in some of their private writings, the Founding Fathers pointed to the Bible as their source of inspiration.

America is the longest thriving form of constitutional government in world history. It is a valid question to ask why America's Constitution has survived so long while governments formed under the influence of irreligion have resulted in upheaval and instability. While many examples could be produced, France alone produces a vivid example. With the French Revolution beginning in 1789, the godless influence of Voltaire and Rousseau have resulted in nearly twenty constitutions in the political life of France compared to America's one Constitution. This should come as little surprise to those who are aware of the personal tumult of these patron saints of French infidelity. The irreligion of succeeding generations of Europeans is directly attributable to this era and the influence of these irreligious infidels.

About the Author and Translator

While this work does not truly concern itself with the primary religious origin of the American Revolution, it does detail the secondary originating principles. What is related by the author is the effect of biblical Christianity upon the American Revolution compared to the godless tyrannical influences that exercised themselves upon the French Revolution.

Friedrich Gentz (Friedrich von Gentz, 1764—1832) was the author of *The Origin and Principles of the American Revolution Compared with the Origin and Principles of the French Revolution*. Mr. Gentz first published this work in German as an essay in a Berlin periodical, titled the *Historic Journal*—a periodical which he founded and which lasted only two or three years.

Gentz had been educated at the University of Königsberg where he fell under the influence of philosopher Immanuel Kant. At the outbreak of the French Revolution, Gentz was at first aroused to its support, but soon converted to more conservative views. Standing against France, Gentz came to assume and espouse the views of Irish statesman and philosopher, Edmund Burke. Burke expressed his own opposition to the French Revolution in his work, *Reflections on the Revolution in France*. So deeply impressed with Burke's *Reflections*, Gentz translated the work into German in 1794—which was the first of Gentz literary endeavors.

Not long after the German publication of *The Origin and Principles of the American Revolution Compared* by Gentz, John Quincy Adams (1767-1848) translated it into English. John Quincy Adams, the son of John Adams, was elected the sixth President of the United States in the election of 1824.

Prior to his election as president, Mr. Adams served his country as a diplomat and politician, something to which he was accustomed from his youth when he accompanied his father as a diplomate to Europe. In 1794, when John Quincy was twenty-seven years of age, President Washington appointed him U.S. ambassador to the Netherlands. In 1796, Mr. Washington appointed him ambassador to Portugal. Later that year, his father was elected president, and he was reassigned as ambassador to Prussia in 1797. As ambassador to Prussia, John Quincy met Friedrich Gentz in Berlin about the time the article first appeared in the *Historic Journal*.

FRIEDRICH VON GENTZ

Prior to sending his translation to America for publication of this work, Mr. Adams attempted to have his translation published in England, but the British were apparently not enthusiastic about publishing a work that reminded them of their loss in the American Revolution. But, in a letter written in the summer of 1800, Mr. Adams notified Gentz of his intention to share his translation with his fellow countrymen in America:

> Berlin, June 16, 1800
> Sir:
> I had already perused with great pleasure the comparison between the origin and principles of the French and American revolutions contained in the Historic Journal for the two last months, before receiving the copies which you had the goodness to send me yesterday. It cannot but afford a gratification to every American attached to the honor of his country to see its revolution so ably vindicated from the imputation of having originated, or been conducted upon the same principles as that of France, and I feel myself as an American citizen highly obliged

to you for the consideration you have bestowed upon the subject, as well as for the honorable manner in which you have borne testimony to the purity of principle upon which the revolution of my country was founded. I beg you, sir, to accept my best thanks for your very acceptable present and to be assured that I shall take much satisfaction in transmitting and making known the treatise to persons in the United States capable of estimating its merits.[5]

JOHN QUNINCY ADAMS

In his hope for an American printing of his translation, Mr. Adams was not disappointed. That same year it was published in Philadelphia as, *The Origin and Principles of the American Revolution, Compared with the Origin and Principles of the French Revolution*. Translated from the German of Gentz; By an American Gentleman. Philadelphia: Published by Asbury Dickins, Opposite Christ-Church. H. Maxwell, Printer, Columbia-House. 1800.

A NOTE CONCERNING THOMAS PAINE

Thomas Paine is regarded as one of America's Founding Fathers, primarily for penning two pamphlets—*Common Sense* (1776) and a pamphlet series titled, *The American Crisis* (1776–1783). Following the American War of Independence, Paine returned to England where he had been raised before making his way to France in 1790. In France, Paine became imbued with the godless sentiments that gave rise to the horrors of the French Revolution. As a result, his latter writing of *Age of Reason* was filled with anti-Christian sentiments.

Late in life, Paine returned to America where he was rejected for his anti-Christian beliefs. It was a common practice of Thomas Paine to seek the advice of Mr. Franklin concerning his early political writings; it appears Paine also sought Franklin's advice concerning the publication of the anti-Christian *Age of Reason*. Mr. Franklin was quite candid in his response.

THOMAS PAINE

> I have read your manuscript with some attention. By the argument it contains against a particular Providence, though you allow a general Providence, you strike at the foundations of all religion. For without the belief of a Providence, that takes cognizance of, guards, and guides, and may favor particular persons, there is no motive to worship a Deity, to fear his displeasure, or to pray for his protection... I would advise you, therefore, not to attempt unchaining the tiger, but to burn this piece before it is seen by any other person; whereby you will save yourself a great deal of mortification by the enemies it may raise against you, and perhaps a good deal of regret and repentance. If men are so wicked with religion [Christianity], what would they be if without it?[6]

Among the other Founding Fathers who opposed Paine was Elias Boudinot. Mr. Boudinot was a Princeton-trained lawyer who, during the years of the American Revolution, became a member of the American spy-network known as the Committee of Correspondence. During the War, he served as one of the Presidents of Congress as well as a delegate to Congress. Following the Revolution, he was elected from New Jersey to the United States House of Representatives to serve in the First, Second, and Third Congresses (from March 4, 1789 to March 3, 1795), but he refused to be renominated for the Fourth Congress. The same year he stepped down from Congress, President Washington nominated him as the second Director of the Mint, in which capacity he served from 1795 to 1805. And, like most Founding Fathers, Elias was concerned about the perpetuation of America upon the Christian principles on which it had been founded. After many local Bible societies had been established throughout America, Elias, John Jay—the first Chief Justice of the Supreme Court—and other Founding Fathers formed the first national Bible society, known as the American Bible Society. Mr. Boudinot became its first president, followed by Chief Justice John Jay.

ELIAS BOUDINOT

Like most of America's Founding Fathers, Elias Boudinot was a deeply dedicated Bible-believing Christian. So offensive was Paine's *Age of Reason* to Mr. Boudinot that he penned his own response. He titled his response, *The Age of Revelation, or, the Age of Reason Shewn to Be an Age of Infidelity*,[7] a direct attack upon Paine's deistic rationalism.

Present-day secularists champion Thomas Paine as a true representative of the American Revolution. But, holding this position is either a confession of their ignorance concerning the disapproval of other Founding Fathers concerning the-latter Thomas Paine or is a deliberate attempt to hide historical reality.

As will be seen below in this work, Thomas Paine was not highly regarded by the author, Friedrich Gentz. And, given John Quincy Adam's approbation of Mr. Gentz, it may be asserted Mr. Adams—who was himself a deeply committed Christian—had no appreciation for Paine's Deism.

POLITICAL VS RELIGIOUS OBSERVATIONS

The fact that Gentz fails to identify the Christian influence upon the American Revolution is not a matter that is easily interpreted. America's Founding Fathers understood that the foundation upon which they sought to establish their nation was the Christian Faith. In a letter to his cousin, Rev. Zabdiel Adams of Lunenburg, Massachusetts (dated June 21, 1776), John Adams wrote...

> Statesmen my dear Sir, may plan and speculate for Liberty, but it is Religion and Morality alone, which can establish the Principles upon which Freedom can securely stand. . . . The only foundation of a free Constitution, is pure Virtue, and if this cannot be inspired into our People, in a greater Measure, than they have it now, they may change their Rulers, and the forms of Government, but they will not obtain a lasting Liberty.—They will only exchange Tyrants and Tyrannies.—You cannot therefore be more pleasantly, or usefully employed than in the Way of your Profession, pulling down the Strong Holds of Satan.[8]

John Adams knew Christian morality was essential to the enjoyment of the highest degree of social freedom that was possible. He believed that the advocates of American independence were united under the principles of Christianity. Years after the letter quoted above was written, John Adams reflected upon the struggle for freedom during the War of Independence, saying…

JOHN ADAMS

> The general principles, on which the [Founding] Fathers achieved independence, were the only principles in which, that beautiful assembly of young gentlemen could unite, and these principles only could be intended by them in their address, or by me in my answer. And what were these general principles? I answer, the general principles of Christianity, in which all those sects [or Christian denominations] were united; and the general principles of English and American liberty, in which all those young men united, and which had united all parties in America, in majorities sufficient to assert and maintain her independence.[9]

John Quincy Adams also understood the important role the Christian Faith played in the founding of America as an independent nation:

> From the day of the Declaration, the people of the North American union, and of its constituent states, were associated bodies of civilized men and Christians, in a state of nature, but not of anarchy. They were bound by the laws of God, which they all, and by the laws of the gospel, which they nearly all, acknowledged as the rules of their conduct. They were bound by the principles which

they themselves had proclaimed in the Declaration.[10]

Why did Mr. Gentz completely overlook the influence of vibrant Christianity upon the rise of America? It is likely that the deeper truth was not convenient to him, any more than it is convenient to many Americans today. From young manhood, Gentz allowed himself to develop a "taste for wine, women and gambling, which pursued him through life".[11] Is it possible that a poignant recognition of the claims of Christianity upon a nation might only serve as an accusation for anyone unwilling to apply similar claims to himself? May we not assume, and even assert, that the principles which Mr. Gentz recognized to produce greater virtue in the American cause is also a greater spring of personal virtue and wellbeing? If those principles are a blessing to a nation, will they not also be so to the individual?

About This Edition

Only the most minor editorial changes have been made throughout this work. While Mr. Adams attempted to reduce the number of "Germanisms"[12] or idioms of the German language in his translation, it is evident that the language and linguistic expressions are far from contemporary. And, I have only made the most minor updates in punctuation—though not bringing the work up to contemporary standards. I have sought only to remove some of the glaring differences that make the work unnecessarily obtrusive to the contemporary reader.

It may be further observed that notes throughout the work are evidently provided by Gentz himself, and not Mr. Adams. Reason to interpret the notes as provided by Gentz is suggested by the use of first person in latter notes.

—Stephen A. Flick, PhD

Preface

A Word from John Quincy Adams

The essay, of which a translation is here given, was published in the *Historic Journal*, a monthly print which appears at Berlin; and was written by Mr. Gentz, one of the most distinguished political writers in Germany. It is for two reasons highly interesting to Americans: First, because it contains the clearest account of the rise and progress of the Revolution which established their independence, that has ever appeared within so small a compass; and secondly, because it rescues that Revolution from the disgraceful imputation of having proceeded from the same principles as that of France. This error has nowhere been more frequently repeated, nowhere of more pernicious tendency than in America itself. It has been, here not simply

JOHN QUNINCY ADAMS

a commonplace argument, as Mr. Gentz represents it to have been in Europe, but has been sanctioned by the authority of men, revered for their talents, and who at least ought to have known better.

The essential difference between these two great events, in their *rise*, their *progress*, and their *termination*, is here shown in various lights, one of which alone is sufficient for an honest man. A modern philosopher may contend that the sheriff, who executes a criminal, and the highwayman, who murders a traveler, act upon the same principles; the plain sense of mankind will still see the same difference between them, that is here proved between the American and French Revolutions— the difference between *right* and *wrong*.

We presume it will afford a pure and honest gratification to the mind of every truly patriotic American reader, to see the honorable testimony borne by an ingenious, well-informed, and impartial foreigner to the principles and conduct of our country's Revolution. The judgment of a native American will naturally be biased by those partialities in favor of his country, from which it is so difficult for the citizen to divest himself as an historian. The causes of hatred and affection must be more remote from the mind of a foreigner, and his decisions must therefore have a greater intrinsic value. The historian of his own country must always in some sort be considered as its advocate; but an impartial foreigner is its judge.

The approbation of such a writer as Mr. Gentz is the more precious too, for not being unqualified. The mild censure, which he passes upon certain parts of our proceedings is the strongest proof of his real impartiality; and though our sentiments as Americans may differ from his, upon various points of political speculation, we shall find very few, if any instances, that have incurred his censure, which our own candor will not equally disapprove.

AMERICAN AND FRENCH REVOLUTIONS COMPARED

Origin and Principles

By Friedrich Gentz

The Revolution of North America, had, in the course of events, been the nearest neighbor to that of France. A very considerable part of those, who were contemporaries and witnesses of the latter had likewise survived the former. Some of the most important personages, who made a figure in the French Revolution, scarce ten years before, had been active on the theatre of that in America. The example of this undertaking, crowned with the most complete success, must have had a more immediate and powerful influence upon those, who destroyed the old government of France, than the example of any earlier European Revolution: the circumstances, in which France was, at the breaking out of her Revolution, had been, if

FRIEDRICH VON GENTZ

not wholly, yet for the greatest part brought on by the part she had taken in that of America. In the conduct and language of most of the founders of the French Revolution, it was impossible not to perceive an endeavor to imitate the course, the plans, the measures, the forms, and, in part, the language of those, who had conducted that of America; and to consider this, upon all occasions, as at once the model, and the justification of their own.

From all these causes, but especially because the recollection of the American Revolution was yet fresh in every mind; because the principles to which it had given currency still sounded in every ear; because the preparatory temper of mind, which it had everywhere in Europe excited and left behind, favored every similar, or only seemingly similar undertaking, it became so easy for those, who felt an evident interest in seeing the French Revolution superficially compared, and thereby placed on the same ground, and confounded with that of America, to draw the great majority of the public into this fundamentally false point of view. At the period of great commotions, and of animated, vehement, widely grasping discussions, a very small number of men are able, and, perhaps, a still smaller number willing, with vigorous native energy, to penetrate into the essence of events, and take upon themselves the painful task of forming a judgment founded upon long meditation and persevering study. The similarity of the two revolutions was taken upon trust, and as many persons of respectable understanding and discernment had loudly and decisively declared themselves in favor of the American, it became a sort of accredited common-place, "that what had been just in America, could not be unjust in Europe." As, further, the last result of the American Revolution had been in the highest degree splendid and glorious; as its issue had been undoubtedly advantageous for America, undoubtedly advantageous for most other states, was undoubtedly advantageous for England herself; as this most important circumstance, and the greater moderation and impartiality which time and tranquility always bring to the judgments of men, had at last reconciled with this Revolution its most violent opponents; an irresistible analogy seemed to justify a similar expectation in respect to that of France; and a second commonplace, far more dangerous than the first, because it seized its materials, in the empty space of distant futurity, gathered a great portion of the human race under the spell of the delusive hope, that "what in America, had conduced to the public benefit, will, and must, sooner or later, in France and throughout Europe conduce in like manner to the public benefit."

The melancholy experience of ten disastrous years, has indeed considerably cooled down this belief; but it is not yet altogether extinguished; and even those who, have begun to totter in the faith, without, however, renouncing the principles, by which they justify the French Revolution, extricate themselves from their perplexity, by recurring to external and accidental circumstances, which have hindered all the good that might have ensued, to the pretense that the Revolution is not yet wholly completed, and to other equally nugatory subterfuges. The justice of the origin of both revolutions, they suppose to be taken for granted; and if one of them has produced more salutary consequences than the other, they impute this to Fortune, which here favors, and there abandons the undertakings of men. An equality of wisdom in the founders of the two revolutions, upon the whole, is as much taken for granted, as an equality of integrity.

Hence, it will certainly be no ungrateful task to compare the two revolutions in their essential features, in their originating causes, and in their first principles with each other. But in order to prepare the way for such a comparison, it will not be superfluous to exhibit in a small compass, the principal features of the origin of the American Revolution. It may justly be taken for granted, that since the last ten years have almost exhausted all the powers of attention and of memory, the characteristic features of the origin and first progress of that revolution are no longer distinctly present in the minds even of many of its contemporaries: there are, besides, some points in the picture of this great event, which, at the time when it happened, escaped almost every observer; and which, not until a later period, discovered themselves in all their vivid colors to the piercing eyes of meditation and experience.[13]

The English colonies in North America, far from being a designed regular institution of European wisdom, calculated for futurity, had been much more the pure production of European short-sightedness and injustice. Political and religious intolerance, political and religious convulsions, had driven the first settlers from their country: the single favor indulged them was to leave them to themselves. That their establishments were, in less than two hundred years, to form a great nation, and to give the world a new form, was concealed no less to their own eyes, than to the eyes of those who had ejected them from their bosom.

In the apparent insignificance of those settlements, and in the false measure, by which the profound ignorance of the Europeans estimated the value of such distant possessions, lay the first ground of the extraordinary progress which the North American colonies had already made under the second and third generations of their new inhabitants. Gold and silver alone could then attract the attention of European governments. A distant land, where neither of these was to be found, was, without hesitation, abandoned to its fortunes. From such a country was expected no *revenue*; and what increases not immediately the revenues of the state, could make no pretensions to its support, or to its particular care.

Nevertheless, by the peculiar, creative energy of a rapidly growing mass of enterprising and indefatigably active men, favored by an extensive, fruitful, and happily situated territory; by simple forms of government, well adapted to their ends, and by profound peace, these colonies, thus neglected, and well-nigh forgotten by the mother country, sprang up, after a short infancy, with giant strides, to the fullness and consistency of a brilliant youth. The phenomenon of their unexpected greatness, roused the Europeans, with sudden violence, from the slumber of a thoughtless indifference, and, at length, displayed to them a real new world, fully prepared to rivalize with the old; for which, however, at the same time, it was an inexhaustible source of wealth and enjoyment. Even before the middle of this century, every maritime power of Europe, but England more than all the rest, because the foundation of her colonies had accidentally departed the least from good principles, had discovered, that the peculiar, and only worth of all external European possessions, consisted in the extended market they opened to the industry of the mother country; that it was not the empty sovereignty over enormous territories; not the barren right of property to gold and silver mines; but solely the increased facility of sale for European productions, and an advantageous exchange of them for the productions of the most distant regions, which gave to the discovery of America the first rank among all the events beneficial to the world.

No sooner had this great truth begun to be so much as obscurely perceived, than necessarily all the exertions of the mother country concentrated themselves, in giving to their trade with the colonies the greatest extent, and the most advantageous direction; and for this end, even in times so little remote from the present, as those of which I speak, no other means were devised, than a *monopoly*. In compelling the inhabitants of the colonies to receive exclusively from the mother country, all the necessary European articles they required, and to sell exclusively to her all the productions, by the circulation of which the merchants of the mother country might hope a certain profit, it was supposed that vast market, whose importance became more evident from year to year, would be improved in its whole extent, and under the most profitable conditions.

The error, which lay at the bottom of this system was pardonable. The genuine principles of the nature and sources of wealth, and of the true interests of commercial nations had scarcely yet germed in a few distinguished heads, and were not even developed, much less acknowledged. Nay, if at that early period, a single state could have soared to the elevation of these principles; on one side; had renounced all prejudices, on the other, every paltry jealousy, and felt a lively conviction, that liberty and general competition must be the basis of all true commercial policy, and the wisest principle of trade with the colonies, yet could she not, without sacrificing herself, have listened to this principle. For in leaving her colonies free, she would have run the risk of seeing them fall into the hands of another, who would exclude her from their market. She was not privileged to be wise alone, and to have expected a general concert among the commercial powers would have been folly. As therefore a colonial trade, grounded upon monopoly, was yet better than none, there remained for a state, in the situation of England, even had she most fortunately anticipated the result of a long experience, and of profound meditation, no other system than that of *monopoly*.

To secure to herself the exclusive trade of the colonies was under these circumstances necessarily the highest aim of England's policy. The establishment of this exclusive trade, which naturally arose from the original relations between the colonies and the mother country, had not been difficult to the state;

for the emigrants had never received the smallest support. By so much the more expensive had it been to keep them. The possession of the colonies was the occasion of wars.

The war of eight years between France and England, which concluded in the year 1763, by the peace of Fontainebleau, and which increased the English national debt nearly an hundred million sterling, had the colonial interest for its sole object. The conquest of Canada would not in itself have been worth a tenth part of the sums, which that war cost; the firm establishment of the commercial monopoly was properly the final purpose, for which they were expended.

It is a great question, whether even independent of the unhappy differences, which broke out immediately after the close of that war, its consequences would not have been rather pernicious than salutary to England. The annihilation of the French power in North America completed the political existence of the English colonies, and supported by the still accelerating progress of their wealth, and of their vigor, gave them a consciousness of security and of stability, which must have become sooner or later dangerous to their connection with the mother country. It is more than improbable that this connection would have been perpetual. It is difficult to believe that under the most favorable circumstances it would have lasted another century. No nation governed its colonies upon more liberal and equitable principles than England; but the unnatural system, which chained the growth of a great people to the exclusive commercial interest of a country, distant from them a thousand leagues, even with the most liberal organization of which it was capable, could not have lasted forever.[14] Yet it would certainly have maintained itself for the next fifty years, and might perhaps have been dissolved in a milder and happier way than has now happened, had not England, under the most wretched of fascinations, fallen upon the idea of procuring in addition to the benefit of an exclusive trade, another immediate benefit, by an American public revenue.

It is hard to decide, which of the secret motives, which on either side were imputed to the ministry of that time first gave existence to this pernicious project. The most pardonable of all, the wish of alleviating the burden of taxes upon the people of Great Britain, and especially upon the land-holders; a burden, which the war had so much aggravated, is unluckily at the same time the most improbable. Specie— was exactly that in which North America least abounded; to have levied in that country a tax of any real importance could scarcely have occurred to any Englishman with the least smattering of information; and that, amidst the thousand obstacles which must necessarily have opposed the collection of such a tax, its net produce for the treasury would always have melted to nothing, could scarcely escape the sagacity of any person versed in the subject. If we consider it attentively on all sides; if we carefully remark certain expressions of the ministers of that day, and what were afterwards known to be their favorite ideas, as well as the whole course of transactions upon American affairs, we can hardly avoid the belief, that what is generally considered as the *consequence* of the first treasury plan, the jealousy of the Parliament's unlimited supremacy was rather the proper motive for this plan; and the secret apprehension that America might grow weary of her fetters, misled them to the dangerous experiment of fastening still narrower chains upon her.

The first step in this untrodden career was taken immediately after the peace of 1763, and under the most unfavorable auspices. The minister of finance, George Grenville, else in every respect an estimable and excellent statesman, but whose mind was either not great or not flexible enough to consider the new system in all its points of view, thought he could force down its execution, just at the period when, by various severe acts of Parliament, he had brought back the commercial relations between England and the colonies as close as possible to the principles of monopoly; had pursued the American contraband trade, with the most oppressive regulations, and thereby had excited a great discontent in all minds. The tax with which he proposed to make his first essay, was a stamp-tax upon judicial records, newspapers, etc. to which the Parliament, at the commencement of the year 1765, gave its assent.

The colonies had hitherto paid no other taxes, than those, which were necessary for the internal administration; and these proportionably insignificant charges had been prescribed and assessed by the several representative assemblies of each colony. In cases of urgency, for instance, in the course of the late war, these assemblies had raised, and presented to the government, extraordinary and voluntary contributions; but of a public tax, raised by act of Parliament, there had been in North America no example. If the Parliament, in the laws regulating trade, had sometimes introduced a trifling entrance, or clearance duty, the most distant trace had never appeared in any public transaction, of a design to make America contribute immediately to the general exigencies of the British empire.

A long and venerable *observance* had sanctioned this colonial immunity; a thousand equitable considerations, and this above all, that the British commercial monopoly was of itself equivalent to a heavy and invaluable tax, justified this observance; and what was most important of all, even the authority of the Parliament to violate this immunity, was controvertible with weapons furnished by the spirit of the English constitution itself. It had always been a favorite maxim of this constitution, that no Briton could be compelled to pay taxes, not imposed by his own representatives, and upon this maxim rested the whole constitutional power of the lower house in Parliament. That the inhabitants of the colonies, in every sense of the word, were Britons, no man questioned; and the Parliament, which thought itself authorized to tax them, even in that, recognized them as fellow citizens. Yet had they no representatives in Parliament, and, owing to their distance, could properly make no pretensions to it. If, therefore, in respect to them, the constitutional principle retained its force, their contributions could only be prescribed by their colonial assemblies, and the British Parliament was no more entitled to exercise the right of taxation over them, than over the people of Ireland.

But had this right been only questionable, it was at all events a false and hazardous step to bring it into discussion. To raise a controversy, concerning the bounds of the supreme power in the state, without the most urgent necessity, is in every case contrary to the simplest rules of state policy. Doubly dangerous must such a controversy here be, where it concerned a constitution, whose nature and boundaries had never yet been defined, and were, perhaps, not susceptible of definition. The relation between a colony and the mother country is one of those, which will not bear a strong elucidation; rights of sovereignty, of so peculiar and extraordinary a nature often vanishes under the hands of those, who would dissect them. Now, when the mother country has a constitution like that of Britain, it becomes infinitely difficult to introduce into that relation a harmony, which satisfies the understanding, and at the same time the idea of right. It had never been examined how far the legislative authority of Parliament, in respect to the colonies, extended; thus much, however, the colonies admitted, and would have continued long to admit, that the Parliament was fully authorized to direct and to restrain their trade, in the widest extent of the word. This alone was clear; but this alone was essential to England. An attempt to go further was manifestly to set all at stake.

The appearance of the Stamp Act in America was the signal for a universal commotion. The new laws against contraband trade had already irritated the minds of the people, because they plainly manifested the purpose of maintaining the British commercial monopoly in its greatest vigor; but these laws were received in silence, because there was no pretention to the right of complaining against them. Now, a new, and hitherto unexampled system, that of raising in North America a tax for the treasury of England, was to be introduced, and in a form necessarily odious to the colonies; for a stamp-tax, from various local causes, had always been in North America an oppressive tax. The opposition spread in a few days among all classes of people; in the lower, it burst forth in excesses of every kind; in the higher, by a stubborn and deliberate resistance, especially by a general agreement to import no merchandize from Great Britain, until the Stamp Act should be repealed. With the temper, which prevailed from one end of the colonies to the other, and with the well-known perseverance, bordering upon obstinacy, of the author of the project, perhaps this first struggle might have ended in the total separation, had not just at that time the administration in England fallen into other hands.

The ministry, which in the summer of 1765, took the affairs of the nation in hand, rejected the new system of immediate taxation in America entirely. The mild principles, and the popular maxims of the Marquis of Rockingham, made him averse to a path, in which violence alone could lead to the goal; and the Secretary of State, General Conway, had been, when the business was first transacted in Parliament, Grenville's most powerful and ardent opposer. The Stamp Act, in the first session of the year 1766, was repealed; but to preserve the honor of Parliament from sinking altogether, with this repeal was connected a declaratory act, intituled, "An Act for securing the Dependence of the Colonies;" in which the right of Great Britain to legislate for the colonies in all cases whatsoever, was solemnly maintained.

This last step could not, in itself, be indifferent to the Americans; yet the joy at the repeal of the Stamp Act was so great, that no regard was paid to the possible consequences of the act, which was attached as a counterbalancing weight to this appeal; and probably peace and concord would have been for a long time restored and secured, had not the English ministry, in a luckless hour, brought again to light the fatal project of raising a revenue from America. The Marquis of Rockingham's administration had been dissolved, soon after the repeal of the Stamp Act, and had been succeeded by another, at the head of which was indeed the name, but no longer the genius of the Earl of Chatham. Charles Townsend, Chancellor of the Exchequer, a man of splendid talents, but of a frivolous and unsafe character, who was aiming to attain the highest summit of influence in the state, when an early death snatched him away from the career, proposed, in the year 1767, a tax upon the importation of glass, paper, painters' colors and tea into the colonies, and this proposal, although several of the ministers, and among the rest the Duke of Grafton, who was at the head of the treasury department had silently contended against it, was by Parliament adopted as a law. The defenders of this new plan entrenched themselves behind the feeble argument, that although Parliament, by repealing the Stamp Act, had renounced a direct taxation of the colonies, yet no renunciation could thence be inferred of indirect taxation, which was intimately connected with the right of regulating trade.

Had this reasoning even silenced the opposition in Parliament, it was by no means calculated to satisfy the colonies. The hostile object of the new statute could not escape the shortest sight. The taxes prescribed, being announced merely as impost duties, were indeed reconcilable with the letter of that immunity, which lays so near the heart of the colonists, but their secret object could scarcely be any other, than to wrest by artifice, what was not ventured to be maintained by force. The insignificance of the benefit England could derive from these taxes, which would have produced only about £20,000, but too strongly confirmed this suspicion; and the peculiar character of the new regulations, the iniquity of exacting from a people, compelled to receive all the articles they needed, exclusively from the mother country, a tax upon the importation of such articles, rendered the undertaking completely odious. The imposts of 1767 operated in exactly the same manner as the Stamp Act; the general non-importation agreement was renewed in all the colonies; bitter controversies between the colonial assemblies and the royal governors, violent scenes between the citizens of divers towns and the military, resistance on the one part, menaces on the other foreboded the stroke, which was soon to shake the British empire to its foundations.

The ministry seemed however to make one more stand, upon the very border of the precipice. In the year 1769, by a circular letter of the minister for the colonies, the pleasing prospect of a speedy relief from the odious impost duties was opened to the colonial assemblies, and the decided aversion of the Duke of Grafton to the taxation of America, seemed to encourage the hopes which this letter had raised. But no sooner had he, in the beginning of 1770, resigned his office, than the affair took another turn. His successor, Lord North, did indeed in the first days of his administration formally propose the repeal of the American imposts, but with the unfortunate exception, that the tax upon tea should be continued as a proof of the legitimate authority of Parliament; nor could the most vehement opposition of the united Rockingham and Grenville parties, who painted in the strongest colors the folly of continuing the contest, after the benefit was abandoned, avail anything against this wretched plan.[15] From that hour it was clear that the ministry had no other object than to make the colonies feel their chains. The first steps in this slippery career had their grounds in false representations and partial judgments; instead of these *errors* dangerous *passions* were now introduced, and the peace and welfare of the nation were to be sacrificed to a mistaken ambition, and a destructive jealousy.

Meanwhile, the disposition to resistance had struck deep roots in all the colonies; and the wider the mother country's undertakings departed from their first object, the more the resistance of the Americans departed from its original character. They had at first only denied the right of Parliament to tax them; by degrees, the sphere of their opposition extended, and they began to call in question the authority of Parliament altogether. When they had once taken this ground, it was in vain to hope to drive them from it. The consciousness of their stability, and their distance from England, their lawful pride in the rights, derived from their British descent, the recollection of the circumstances which had led their forefathers to America, the sight of the flourishing state into which in a period of 150 years they had turned an uninhabitable desert, the injustice, and the harshness of those, who instead of alleviating their dependence by gentle treatment, were daily seeking to render it more oppressive; all this encouraged the new impulse, which their ideas and their wishes had taken. The folly of Great Britain in abandoning, for the useless discussion of a problematic right, the undisturbed enjoyment of a connection, which though never analyzed and dissected with theoretic accuracy, was even in its undefined state so advantageous, became continually more visible; but far from endeavoring with tender caution to heal the dangerous wound, measure upon measure was taken to inflame it. Almost every step taken by the government during this unhappy period, in respect to the internal administration of the colonies, to the courts of justice, to the provincial assemblies, to the relations between the civil and military authorities, seemed expressly calculated at once to embitter and to embolden discontent; and the spirit of insurrection had long been in full possession of every mind, when a new attempt of the ministry, made it suddenly burst forth with the utmost violence.

The persevering refusal of the Americans to import tea into the colonies, so long as the tax upon it, prescribed in the year 1767, and purposely retained in 1770, should not be repealed, had occasioned a considerable loss to the East India Company, in whose magazines, great quantities of this article perished unconsumed. They had offered the minister to pay upon the exportation double the trifling tax of three pence upon the pound, which was yet so odious to the colonies; but this proposal, advantageous as it was, and which opened so honorable an issue from the crisis, was disapproved and rejected, as not according with the system of reducing America to unconditional submission. But as the embarrassment of the company was continually growing greater, they sought to help themselves by another project, and concluded to ship the tea for America upon their own account, there to pay the impost by their own agents and then make their sales. As at the same time, by act of Parliament, the exportation was made duty free, whereby the tea, notwithstanding the impost in America, would be at a cheaper market than it had before been, it was hoped that the Americans would abandon all their scruples, and not feeling immediately the tax lurking in the price of the article, would give up all resistance.

The event soon discovered how vain this hope had been. Time had been allowed the colonies to reflect upon their situation, and to judge of the ministerial proceeding in the point of view which was alone essential. The merchants, who during the American agreement against the importation of British tea, had enriched themselves by the contraband trade of foreign teas, might, perhaps, only from mercantile considerations, abhor the undertaking of the East India company, sanctioned by the government; but the great mass of the people, and the most enlightened patriots in America, saw and condemned, in this undertaking, nothing but the evident purpose of carrying through the taxing right of the British Parliament. The remarkable circumstance, that England had refused the larger revenue, which the taxes upon exportation from the British ports would have produced, to secure the levying of the much smaller entrance duty in America, betrayed a bitter passionate obstinacy, which together with so many other symptoms of hostility threatened the colonies with a gloomy futurity.

When the first report of these tea-ships having been sent arrived in America, from New Hampshire to Georgia, universal preparations for the most animated resistance were made. The agents of the company nowhere dared to receive the goods; in New York, Philadelphia, and many other towns, such strong protestations against unlading the ships were made, that they were compelled to return untouched. In Boston, where the spirit of resistance had been from the beginning the most violent, Governor Hutchinson adopted measures to make the return of the ships impossible before the object should be attained; but his rigor only served to increase the evil. A small number of decided opponents, went on board the ship, and, without doing any other damage, broke open 342 chests of tea, and threw it into the sea.

The account of these tumultuous proceedings, soon after the opening of Parliament, in the year 1774, reached England, where, immediately, the thirst for revenge silenced every other feeling; the zeal to maintain the honor and the rights of government, every other council, not only in the minds of the ministers, but likewise in the general opinion of the nation. In this critical moment it was forgotten, that it was not until after the colonies for ten years long, had been driven by a series of vicious and hazardous measures, by attacks continually repeated, and by studied systematic vexations to the utmost extremity, that their just indignation had burst forth in illegal acts.

The necessity for severe measures was indeed now evident, even to the moderate. But unfortunately, resentment overstepped the bounds of equity, and provoked pride the bounds of policy. The immediate authors of the excesses in Boston, might justly have been punished; the East India Company might justly claim to be indemnified by the colonies; the Americans, by their acts of violence, had evidently placed themselves at a disadvantage; and their faults gave the most favorable opportunity to bring them, with wisdom, back within their bounds. But England seemed herself to spurn all the advantages of her present situation, and to have commenced a war, rather against her own welfare and security, than against the opposition in the colonies. The first measure, proposed by Lord North, was a law, to close as long as the king should think necessary, the port of Boston, and to transfer the custom-house of that flourishing and important commercial town to another place. Immediately after, appeared a second law, which struck still deeper at the vital principle of the colonies, which scarcely could be justified by the most exaggerated ideas of the Parliament's authority, and which could not but unavoidably drive to despair, men, who had already been almost impelled to insurrection by an Impost Tax. This harsh law declared the province of Massachusetts Bay's charter void, and subjected this province, which by its wealth, its constitution hitherto, and the sentiments of its inhabitants, seemed to be more dangerous to the government, than all the rest, to a new organization, grounded on an absolute dependence upon the crown. At the same time, another act of Parliament ordained, that persons, who during the tumults in America, had committed offences against public officers, in every case, where the governor should have reason to apprehend that they could have no impartial trial there, should be sent to England for trial; a statute, which according to British ideas, deserved the epithet of tyrannical. Finally, the minister brought into Parliament a law, giving to the province of Canada, which had been until then under a merely temporary administration, a constitution entirely different from the forms of the other colonial governments; and, however the most recent experience might seem to justify the government in this step, it could not but produce the most unfavorable operation in the colonies, who believed to read their own future destiny in the treatment of that neighboring country.

As soon as these measures were known in America, the general indignation, irritated yet further by the reinforcement of the royal troops in Boston, and by various unpleasant circumstances and oppressions, inseparable from this event, was raised to the highest and most dangerous pitch. Instantaneously, through all the colonies but one voice was heard; that the contest with England could be decided only by the sword. Preparations for the most resolute defense were everywhere the great occupation; exercises of arms became the sole employment of the citizens. A congress of fifty-one deputies from all the provinces assembled on the 4th of September, 1774, at Philadelphia, to consult upon the common grievances, and upon the means of averting the common danger. The first measures of this assembly consisted in a solemn declaration, that the unjust and oppressive proceeding of Parliament against the town of Boston, and the province of Massachusetts Bay, was to be considered as the cause of all the colonies; and in a recommendation to the inhabitants of

North America to suspend all commercial intercourse with Great Britain, until the just grievances of the colonies should be redressed. Hereupon, the congress resolved upon an address to the British nation, and another to the king of England, in which the distressed situation of North America was delineated with boldness and energy, but at the same time with evident moderation, and in a language, which still deprecated a separation from the mother country, as a very great evil.

It could no longer be concealed to the dullest eye, that the contest with the colonies had assumed a new and formidable character, and had spread to such an extent, as threatened the whole British empire. Yet, nothing is more certain, than that at this decisive moment, it still depended upon the Parliament to finish it happily. No resolution, less than that of a total repeal of all the laws, promulgated since 1766, was commensurate with the greatness of the danger; but the thought that the immediate loss of America was at stake, should have reconciled every mind to this only remaining mean of salvation. Unfortunately, the deep exasperation, the inflexible pride, the false ambition, all the angry passions, which this cruel system had introduced and nourished, maintained now likewise their predominance; and a fatal error, the opinion that the victory over the colonies would be infallible and easy, entered into an unholy league with all those passions. The Parliament, at the beginning of the year 1775, in a remarkable address to the king, declared, that both houses, convinced that a formal rebellion had broken out in the province of Massachusetts Bay, would faithfully support him in every measure against rebellious subjects. Immediately afterwards, several laws of unmerciful severity, by which the colonies were deprived of all foreign commerce, and, what was yet harder, even of that fishery upon the coasts of Newfoundland so highly essential to their subsistence, passed by great majorities. Some of the wisest and most venerable statesmen, Lord Chatham,[16] Lord

Camden, Lord Shelburne, in the upper house, Edmund Burke, Colonel Barré, and others in the House of Commons, exerted in vain against these desperate resolutions, all the powers of an astonishing eloquence; such as perhaps had never been surpassed. The several plans of conciliation, which they proposed, were rejected, always with displeasure, sometimes with contempt; the only step towards peace that ever was attempted, rested upon a project of Lord North, evidently incompetent to the end; which would scarcely have satisfied the colonies at the outset of the dispute, and certainly could not content them in the year 1775.

The congress assembled, for the second time, in May, 1775, and declared, "that by the violation of the charter of Massachusetts Bay, the connection between that colony and the crown was dissolved." The conciliatory bills of Lord North were rejected; a *continental army* and a *paper currency* were created; Colonel Washington was appointed commander in chief of the American troops, &c. The war at this period had, in fact, broken out; it had been opened by the battle of Lexington, on the 19th of April, and while the congress was adopting these resolutions, a second and much bloodier action took place at Bunker's hill, where the loss suffered by the English army gave a severe, though unfortunately, a fruitless lesson to those, who had treated with so much contempt the resistance, and the military talents of the Americans.

Although every hope of peace had now well-nigh vanished, the Congress were not however so far discouraged, as to decline venturing, even at this period, a last attempt at conciliation. They resolved a second address to the king, in which the colonies under the most forcible assurances of their submission, and of their unabated wish to remain united with Great Britain, intreated in the most urgent manner, that his majesty would give his assent to any plan whatsoever, calculated to pacify this wretched contest. The address was presented on the 1st. of September 1775, by Mr. Penn, of Pennsylvania, one of the most respectable citizens of North America, who was informed "that no answer would be given to it." Soon after the minister brought into Parliament the law, which prohibited all intercourse with the colonies, and declared their ships to be lawful prize; a law, which was justly considered as a declaration of war against America, and by some as a formal abdication of the right of government over the colonies. At the same time, the king concluded alliances with several German princes, who engaged their troops for a great undertaking; and preparations of every kind announced that force alone was to decide the destiny of the British empire. At the close of the session of Parliament in February 1776, the bitterness had attained its highest pitch. Even the evident danger, that foreign powers, and France in particular, might take a part in the disturbances in America, and take advantage of England's embarrassment, made no impression upon the ministers and the Parliament. When some members of the opposition at the beginning of the year 1776, asserted that according to very authentic accounts, a negotiation between the Congress at Philadelphia, and the French court, was already commenced, not only the truth, but even the possibility of this but too well-grounded fact was denied. It was maintained "that, such an unexampled fascination," could not be supposed in any nation, "holding colonies itself, in any government wishing to retain the obedience of their own subjects." A reasoning, which in itself rested upon very just principles, but which lost all its conclusive weight in the mouth of those, who, by a fascination entirely similar, had come to the point of setting at stake, from mere stupid obstinacy, one of their most precious possessions, and half the existence of their empire.

Since the last months of the year 1775, the war was raging in the bowels of the colonies. The language and the resolves of

Parliament in the winter of 1775-1776, taught the Americans that it would be a war for life and death—every bond of union was broken. Against the return of the old happy days, the iron hand of inexorable destiny had barred every gate. On the 4th of July 1776, the Congress declared the Independence of the Thirteen United States.

It belongs not to the purpose of the present essay to continue further this cursory historical recapitulation, since I am here speaking only of the *origin* of the American Revolution. It is however sufficiently known, that the progress and the issue of the war, completely justified the anticipations of those, who would have avoided it *at any price*. It is equally well known, how much the *consequences* of this war, have put to shame the expectations of all parties. The supporters of the war, went upon the principle, that everything must be hazarded to maintain the possession of the colonies, its opponents, upon the principle that everything must be sacrificed not to lose them; both concurred therefore in the opinion that this loss would give a deep, and perhaps incurable wound to the British empire. Experience has decided. In a few years after the loss of the colonies, England has again become as powerful and flourishing, nay more powerful and flourishing than ever. And, whatever of a hurtful nature, that lay in the influence of this event upon the affairs of Europe, has fallen upon France alone; upon France, who, according to the general opinion, was to derive the greatest advantages from the American Revolution.

If we duly meditate upon the series of facts, which have been here summarily exhibited, and upon some others equally certain and authentic, which will be touched upon in the sequel, the following points of comparison will arise, to show in its clearest light the *essential* difference between the American and French Revolutions.

1. The American Revolution was grounded partly upon principles, of which the right *was evident*, partly upon such, as it was at least very questionable, whether they were not right, and from beginning to end upon no one that was clearly and decidedly wrong; the French Revolution was an uninterrupted series of steps, the wrong of which could not, upon rigorous principles, for a moment be doubted.

The question, concerning the *right* of a revolution, has, by the frivolous way of thinking, by the shallow sophistry, and even by the immense devastations, and the stupid indifference arisen from them, of this revolutionary age, been in a manner discarded among the idle amusements of scholastic pedants; many who hold themselves for statesmen, think it no longer *worthwhile so much as* to start the question; yet in the eyes of the thinking, of the wise and the good, will it ever remain, the first and the last.

The relation between the inhabitants of a distant colony, and the government of the mother country, is never to be compared in all respects with the relation between the government and their immediate subjects. In the former, there lies always something strained, something equivocal, something unnatural; for it cannot be denied, the firmest foundation of all sovereignty is in the wants of the governed, and those wants are weaker, are more questionable, withdraw themselves, to express myself so, from the eyes and the feeling, when the government is a thousand leagues distant from the country, which must obey their laws. Besides, all the European states, which founded, or encouraged the foundation of colonies in the other quarters of the globe, considered these colonies, more or less, as mere instruments to *enrich* and strengthen the seat of their own power, and treated the people, who inhabited them, merely as the means of an happier, or more agreeable existence for their own. A maxim, which could not easily be reconciled with the general purposes of society, for which the colonies must have as keen a sense as the mother country, and with the consciousness of independent stability, to which they must sooner or later attain. Hence, the right of an European nation over their colonies must necessarily always be a wavering, insecure, undefined, and often undefinable right. If, however, the form of government in the mother country be simple, and the conditions, upon which the colony was founded, were in themselves clear and definite, then that unavoidable misrelation will be less perceptible. The difficulties on the other hand must be much greater, the collisions more frequent and momentous, when the mother country has a complicated constitution, and when the conditions under which the colonies are connected with her, the rights, which they enjoy by virtue of her particular constitution, the place which they are to hold in that constitution, are not in the precisest manner defined at their very origin.

This was in both points the case with the English colonies, in North America. How far the rights and liberties of a new state, founded by Britons, under the British constitution, should extend, and in what particular relation the inhabitants of such a state should stand, with the several component parts of that mixed constitution? this was a question, which at their origin should have been considered with the utmost attention. This question was never once thought of. The colonies originated at a time, when the British constitution itself had not yet attained its last perfection and consistence.[17] Their charters all proceeded from the crown. The Parliament had never taken any part in their settlement.

The internal forms of government of these colonies were as various, as the circumstances, under which they had been founded, or formed. Some of the most important had been granted as hereditary property to private persons, so that these, and their heirs, might govern them entirely as they pleased, and were scarcely more than under a nominal dependence upon the crown. In this manner had Maryland been granted to lord Baltimore; North and South-Carolina to lord Clarendon; in this manner Pennsylvania and Delaware belonged to the family of the celebrated Penn. Others, as New-Hampshire, New York, New-Jersey, and Virginia, were called royal provinces, and in these the king was considered as the immediate sovereign. Lastly, there was a third class of colonies, which were called privileged, and in which the power of the monarch was limited by the original charters. Such was the constitution of Massachusetts, of Rhode Island, and of Connecticut.

The relations between the royal governors, and the provincial assemblies, were in every colony differently defined and modified; but the provincial assemblies were accustomed everywhere, whether the province was originally privileged, royal, or hereditary, more or less, to exercise the right of enacting laws for the internal police of the province, of levying taxes for meeting the public exigencies of the state, and of taking an essential part in everything belonging to the administration of the country. In no single colony, however its constitution, in respect to its dependence upon the crown, was organized, was there a trace of a constitutional and legal authority, vested in the British Parliament. The charters contained none; no definite law, not so much as a partial statute, enacted in Great Britain, had ever proclaimed, or even made mention of such an authority.

In the beginning, the Parliament considered this their absolute exclusion from the sovereignty over the colonies with great indifference; in the preceding century, the bounds of their power in general were so little defined, that not the smallest doubt has been started against the authority of the king, at his pleasure to give, to grant, to constitute, to privilege, to govern, by himself, or allow to be governed by others, an immense continent in America; this distant and uncultivated land, was besides far too much despised for them to concern themselves about its constitution. But when, on the one side, after the Revolution of 1688, the influence of Parliament upon all the affairs of government had become greater, firmer, and more general; and when, on the other side, the extraordinary importance of the colonies, in their rapidly growing population, in their constantly improving culture, in their unexpected and splendid flourishing state, was daily more evident, the idea by degrees crept into every mind, that so great and essential a part of the British empire could not possibly be altogether withdrawn from the superintendence of Parliament, even though nothing should have been said of it hitherto in the public transactions.

In one single, though truly important point, the Parliament had always exercised the legislative power over the colonies, in everything which concerned trade, whether of export, or of import. Although this was precisely the seat of that mighty monopoly, which seemed to give the colonies their whole value, and which, on the other side, could never be so favorable to their progress as liberty would have been, yet they willingly submitted to the regulations and restraints of all kinds, with which the Parliament in ample measure provided them. It appeared natural and equitable to themselves, that the supreme legislative power in the empire, should regulate and direct a concern, which interested not exclusively America, but England too, in a much higher degree. The right of the Parliament, therefore, to prescribe laws to the colonies relating to commerce, and to everything connected with it, was never called in question.

But, as soon as the Parliament determined to over-step this right, and to levy taxes in America, without the consent of the local representatives, the most vehement resistance could not fail to break out, and this resistance could as little fail to increase, when, in the progress of the contest, the pretention to bind America by act of Parliament, in all cases whatsoever, was advanced, and formally derived from what was called the legal supremacy of Parliament. The *omnipotence* of Parliament, so often, and so loudly, then resounded by the antagonists of the colonies, was a very just principle for England, but a very invalid one for America. With the Parliament, bating the trade laws, to which the colonists submitted from reason and necessity, America had not the least to do. America sent no representatives to Parliament, nor did it ever occur to Parliament to offer her that power, which would indeed not have been without great difficulties carried into effect. The colonies, nevertheless, possessed all the benefits of the British constitution, and even the greatest part of their forms. Almost in every one of them, there was a *representative assembly*, which supplied the place of a lower house, and a senate, which answered to the house of peers. These assemblies transacted, under the sanction of the monarch, all the affairs, which in England and Ireland were done by the Parliaments. They enacted laws, levied taxes, deliberated upon the exigencies, and upon the administration of their provinces. They formed, in concurrence with the king and his governors, a complete government, organized altogether in the spirit of the English constitution, and needed no co-operation of the British Parliament. The constitutions of the several provinces, knew only the king, and the provincial representative bodies, and had no more reference to the Parliament of Great Britain, than to the Parliaments of France. They had existed more than a century, without knowing anything of the English Parliament, otherwise than by its commercial regulations, which had not always been to them the most agreeable. The pretended right of Parliament to prescribe laws and taxes for them, was an arbitrary assumption, against which the colonies, according to all legal principles, might proceed exactly as Great Britain would have done, had any of the provincial assemblies undertaken, with the concurrence of the king, to levy taxes in England or Scotland, or to overthrow the municipal constitution of London or Westminster, as the Parliament had overthrown the charter of Massachusetts Bay.

The resistance of the colonies, and the unavoidable insurrection, which was finally produced by the continuance of the attack, were, therefore, inasmuch as they respected the Parliament, perfectly *right*. The Parliament was, in regard to the colonies, to be considered as a *foreign power*. So long as this power had remained within the bounds of its silently acknowledged sphere of operation, the colonies had submitted to it. To give laws beyond those bounds, it was as little authorized, as would have been the legislative power of any other nation. The Americans could resist it with the same right, as they might have resisted the States-General of Holland, or the council of the Indies in Madrid, had these undertaken to impose upon them their manufacturing regulations, or stamp taxes.

The question seems to be more difficult, with what right the colonies could likewise resist the king, who, at any rate, was their legal and acknowledged sovereign? But, if in this respect the lawfulness of their conduct be doubtful, it would at least remain a great point, that its unlawfulness could not be clearly proved, and a closer examination will lead us to a result yet far more favorable to the justification of this conduct.

For there is a very evident distinction between an insurrection in a *simple*, and one in a *complicated*, or *mixed constitution*. In a simple government, every resistance against the supreme power, is absolutely illegal, and requires no further examination to be condemned. In a mixed government, cases may be imagined, in which the matter is very intricate, and therefore problematic and dubious.

In a mixed government, the supreme power, or the proper sovereign, consists always of several component parts connected together and regulated by the constitution. Each of these parts has its constitutional rights and prerogatives; and those of any one part, though in themselves more important, cannot be more sacred than those of any other. When either of them exceeds its legal bounds, and oppresses, or endeavors to destroy another, this latter, unless the constitution be an empty name, must have the right of resisting; and, unless the war, arising from this resistance, be not averted by some fortunate expedient; if the old balance cannot again be restored, the contest must necessarily, and legally end with the dissolution of the constitution. For between two independent component parts of the supreme power in a state, there can no more be a judge, than between two independent states. That this is a most unfortunate situation for the whole nation, interested in it, is self-evident. The most dreadful circumstance it brings with it, is unquestionably this, that the people in such a controversy never know whom to obey, and whom to resist; for whom to declare, and against whom to act; that all rights and duties are thrown into confusion, and involved in obscurity, and that it becomes a problem, who is within, and who is without the line of insurrection. This evil is inseparable from mixed forms of government;[18] and however great it may be, its possibility can never be excluded from such constitutions. If, for example, the two houses of the British Parliament should make the attempt to enact laws, without the sanction of the king, or the king, without the concurrence of Parliament, the injured party would beyond all doubt resist, and resist with energy; nor could anyone deny that this resistance, even though it should end in civil war and the ruin of the constitution, was perfectly lawful.

The American colonies were precisely in this, or at least in an extremely similar situation. Their constitution before the Revolution was evidently a monarchy, more or less limited by the influence of their provincial assemblies. The legislative and executive powers were divided between the king and the provincial assemblies, as in England, between the king and the two houses of Parliament. The king and his governor had only a negative upon acts of legislation, and the provincial assemblies in most of the colonies had a considerable share in the government. In all the provinces (Pennsylvania since 1700 excepted) these assemblies were divided into two houses, closely corresponding in their functions, with the two branches of the British Parliament. The lower house, or the representative assembly possessed everywhere the exclusive right of prescribing taxes. In some colonies, for instance, in Maryland, the king, by the charter, had *expressly renounced* all right of taxation. In several others he had, in the literal sense of the word, only reserved the empty title of sovereignty. Connecticut and Rhode Island were perfect democracies. The colonial assemblies of these provinces chose their governors without the confirmation of the king, and dismissed them at pleasure; they allowed no appeals from their courts of justice; their laws required no royal assent; nay, what is more remarkable, and a proof of their absolute independence, their charters granted them even the right of peace and war.

The king's power was, therefore, in all the colonies, more or less limited; in some, to such a degree that it could not be compared with his legitimate power in Great Britain; and the colonial assemblies had a constitutional right to resist him, when he violated their constitutional powers. Now, the measures of the ministry, from 1764, were evident attacks, upon those powers. Whether the Parliament had advised, or confirmed those attacks, was, as we have before shown, nothing to the colonies; they had to do only with the king, and the king, according to their constitutions, could levy no taxes, but such as the provincial assemblies proposed. The Stamp Act of 1764, was, therefore, a violation of their rights; the impost act of 1767, was a violation of their rights; the act of 1770, which maintained the tea-tax to support the supremacy of Parliament, was a gross, and what was worst of all, an insulting violation of their rights. To punish them for their constitutional resistance against these unconstitutional resolves, was a revolting injustice; the mode of punishment (the Boston port-bill, the bill to abolish the Massachusetts charter, &c.) was not merely a violation, it was an entire dissolution of their rights. It was nothing more, than the proclamation of a *fact*, when the congress, in 1775, declared, "that by the abolition of the Massachusetts charter, *the connection between that province and the crown was dissolved*." No resource was left but that of repelling force by force. The convocation of their first congress, was in itself not an illegal measure. This congress exercised originally only the same rights, which were unquestionably within the powers of every provincial assembly. It represented a legal resistance, and sought the means of preserving to America the constitution she had hitherto possessed. It was not until after the ministry had spurned at peace, rejected every proposal of conciliation, and finally required unconditional submission, that is, had *dissolved the constitution*, that the congress proceeded to the declaration, which substituted a new government, in the stead of that which was destroyed.

Had the colonies had the design (and it cannot be denied that they manifested it clearly enough) in this whole contest to separate the king completely from the Parliament, all the means were taken away from them of regulating their conduct, according to a system founded upon such a separation. The most intimate union subsisted between the ministry and the Parliament; nor was it possible to resist the one, without quarrelling with the other. The king confirmed the hostile acts of Parliament; he ceased to be the constitutional monarch of the colonies, and entered into an alliance with those, whom they considered as usurpers in a legal point of view. Had the king of England allied himself with a foreign power (and in a constitutional sense the Parliament was no other to the colonies) against the Parliament of Great Britain, how would it be possible for the Parliament to arm against this foreign power, and yet spare the king of England? Or rather, would not the mere undertaking of such an alliance include within itself an immediate justification of every defensive measure taken by the injured party, and an absolute renunciation of the constitution.

I think I have here sufficiently developed the first point in the comparison I proposed, that which relates to the conduct of North America; there now remains only the easy task of exhibiting the second, which relates to the conduct of France.

The single period of the disturbances in France, when mention was made of militating *rights*, was that in which the Parliaments took part, in 1787 and 1788. If the prerogatives of these Parliaments were not so great and so unquestionable, as they would have represented them, yet their appeal to them gave at least a color of lawfulness to their undertakings. That period, however, is to be considered only as preparatory to the real Revolution.

From the breaking out of this Revolution, the question as to the *lawfulness* of what the popular leaders did, was never (an extraordinary, yet an indubitable fact!) started. The word *right* would have vanished from the French language, had not an imaginary right of the *nation*, to do whatever they, or their representatives should please, appeared as a sort of substitute for all other rights.

This is not the place to analyze this *right of the nation*, sometimes likewise called *right of man*, a sort of magic spell, with which all the ties of nations and of humanity were insensibly dissolved. Those, who were serious in advancing, grounded it upon the chimerical principle of the sovereignty of the people, which I have endeavored upon another occasion to elucidate. Thus, much is certain, that the leaders of the Revolution, under the shelter of this talisman, spared themselves and others the trouble of enquiring into the lawfulness of their proceedings; for in their system, all was right, which they resolved upon in the name of the *people*, or in the name of mankind.

In order to judge of their actions, according to their deserts, they must be snatched away from the tribunal they have erected for themselves, and placed at another bar, whose laws accord better with the dictates of uncorrupted reason, and the eternal prescriptions of *real right*.

When the deputies of the states, assembled together in the year 1789, they had beyond all doubt the *right*, to undertake great reforms in the government, and even in the constitution of the French monarchy. This right, however, they could exercise only under the three following conditions. First, that they should observe the general forms of an assembly of the states in France, until these forms should in a *lawful* manner be abolished, or changed. Secondly, that their laws should not have the force of laws, until assented to by the monarch. And, thirdly, that they should follow the instructions, given them by their constituents.

In less than six weeks, they had broken through these three fundamental conditions. The deputies of the third state, without the least authority, and with a shameful violation of the rights of the other states, declared that themselves alone constituted the national assembly.

When the king endeavored to bring them back from this monstrous usurpation to their proper limits, they declared to him that they persisted in it, formally renounced obedience to him, and reduced him finally to the necessity of commanding the two other estates to acknowledge the usurpation.

That in the immeasurable career, which these two first successful acts of violence, had opened, they might no longer meet resistance from any quarter, they declared that the instructions of their constituents were not binding upon them.

They had proceeded thus far, when, partly by their influence and example, partly by faults of the court, which need not be considered here, where the question only relates to *right*, the general rebellion broke out in Paris, and in all the provinces. Far from *disapproving* this rebellion, which, in perfect contrast with the rising of the people in America, had not the most distant connection with the lawful objects of the national assembly, they cherished and fostered it, gave it legislative force and consistence, conferred civic crowns upon its authors, called it an holy and virtuous insurrection, and took care to have it maintained in a continual flame, during the whole period of their government.

Under the shadow of this insurrection, they, who had placed themselves at its head, and taken upon themselves all responsibility, in a period of two years ran through the most remarkable circle of violation of all rights, public and private, that the world ever beheld. They drew up, without ever so much as *asking the free assent of the king*, a constitution so called, the incompetency, the impracticability, the ridiculous absurdity of which was so great, that, even among its authors— (another unexampled yet indubitable fact) not a single man would ever have seriously defended it. This constitution they compelled the king, upon pain of being immediately dethroned, to subscribe and swear to.

Scarcely had this happened, when their successors, who by virtue of this constitution alone, had a sort of legal existence, and held something resembling an authority to show, instead of governing and quieting the state according to this constitution, directed all their secret, and what was still more revolting, all their public measures to its destruction. In less than a year they succeeded in effecting this new usurpation. Without so much as having a *legal pretext*, they suspended the constitution, dethroned the king, assumed to themselves, still forsooth *in the name of the people*, the power of calling a *national convention*, and proclaimed the republic, with fewer formalities, than a man would use to change his dress. By long habit dead to every sentiment of right, tormented by all the furies, plunged by their frantic measures, by crimes, and calamities of every kind into the lowest depth of criminal foolhardiness, they now proclaimed against humanity and all its rights, a formal, irreconcilable war; and to shut behind them every door for return, and to snap the last thread by which they still held together with a lawful existence, they finally murdered justice herself, in the person of the most conscientious and upright monarch, who had ever adorned a throne.

The French Revolution, therefore, began by a violation of rights, every step of its progress was a violation of rights, and it was never easy, until it had succeeded to establish absolute wrong, as the supreme and acknowledged maxim of a state completely dissolved, and yet existing only in bloody ruins.

2. The American Revolution was from beginning to end, on the part of the Americans, merely a *defensive Revolution*; the French was from beginning to end, in the highest sense of the word, an *offensive Revolution*.

This difference of itself is essential and decisive; upon it rests, perhaps more than upon any other, the peculiar character, which has distinguished these two Revolutions.

The British government began the Revolution in America by resolves, for which they could show no right; the colonies endeavored by all means in their power to repel them. The colonies wished to maintain their old constitution; the government destroyed it. The resistance, which the colonies opposed against the mother country, was, in every period of this unhappy contest, exactly commensurate with the attack; the total separation was not resolved, until the utter impossibility of preserving the ancient condition was proved.

The Stamp Act threw America into the most violent commotion; tumultuous scenes, though attended with no acts of bloody violence, broke out in all the provinces.[19] But they were nowhere formally sanctioned by the approbation of the legislative authorities. The little congress of 28 deputies of several colonies, who in the year 1765 assembled at New York, and served as the model for the subsequent larger assembly, passed no other resolution than that "the colonies could only be taxed by their representatives," and expressed this perfectly lawful resolve, in *petitions* to the king. The single general measure, which was then offered, the non-importation agreement, was a voluntary engagement, sanctioned by no public authority.

The *Declaratory Act*, which appeared in the year 1766, together with the repeal of the stamp-tax, could not possibly be agreeable to the colonies since it expressly and solemnly maintained the right of the British Parliament to bind them by law in all cases whatsoever. Yet was this act received with great and remarkable tranquility; and had the British government, from that time forward, given up forever their unhappy innovations; had they continued to govern the colonies, according to the old constitutional principles, there never would have been uttered a complaint against the declaratory act. It was long afterwards, and when the colonies had been provoked by repeated attacks of every kind, to the utmost extremity, that the provincial assembly of Massachusetts Bay, declared that statute, an oppression.

The resistance against the Impost Taxes of 1767, was of the same nature, as that which the stamp-tax had experienced. This new grievance of the colonies, was accompanied with circumstances of the most odious kind: the augmentation of the troops, the conduct of a part of them, the harshness of some governors, the frequent adjournments and violent dissolution of the provincial assemblies, all was calculated to put the patience of the Americans to dangerous proof. And yet they never overstepped the boundaries, which the constitution and the laws prescribed to them; and in their numerous addresses and protestations, adhered rigorously to what was allowed by law. When in the year 1770, a violent quarrel arose between some of the royal soldiers, and certain citizens of Boston, which ended in the first bloody scene the colonies had in their contest with England yet witnessed, the courts of law, with a glorious impartiality, acquitted the greatest part of the accused and indicted soldiers.

The continuation of the tax upon tea in the year 1770, had no other consequence than to strengthen the voluntary agreement against the importation of English tea; the resolve in the year 1773, which authorized the East India Company to the exportation of their stores of tea, free from duty, and the actual execution of this resolve, could not, indeed but produce a still more unfavorable operation. This measure was altogether calculated to provoke the colonies to a general insurrection. Yet did they keep themselves rigorously within the limits of a necessary defense. The destruction of the tea at Boston was, in fact, no other than a defensive operation. The sale of this tea, or only a part of it, would have involved the compulsive levy of a tax, by the payment of which the constitution of the colonies and all their rights would have been lost. Yet, even then, they proceeded not beyond what was unavoidable, and measured the resistance as exactly as possible by the attack. The tea was thrown into the sea, and not a single hostile step followed upon this undertaking. Nay, although the public authorities of Boston, and of the whole province, held it for necessary, as much as every single citizen, yet they always undeniably discovered themselves ready to grant the fullest indemnity to the East India Company.

Had the ministry, at this period, been contented with an equitable satisfaction; had they, if they must punish, been content to inflict tolerable and proportionable punishments, there is no doubt but America would have remained with her old constitution. Although a great part of the inhabitants of the colonies, in expectation of a distressing and stormy futurity, urged for energy and for arming, yet was this temper still far from being common. It is, for example, a certain fact, that in the important province of Pennsylvania, the majority of the citizens would have voted against taking a part in the measures at Boston, had not the excessive and unwise harshness of the Parliament, in a short time, inflamed and united all minds.

The appearance of the act, which closed the port of Boston, of that which, immediately after, took away the Massachusetts charter, the account of all what had passed in Parliament upon that occasion, the visible impossibility of eradicating peaceably such deep rooted bitterness—all these circumstances concurred to render a sudden explosion probable; many of the resolves of Parliament were indisputably of a nature to furnish sufficient motive for such an explosion. But the provincial assemblies contented themselves with sending deputies to a general congress. Not one over hasty step disturbed the pacific and lawful character of their conduct in this hard and trying period.

The congress, which assembled at Philadelphia, spoke with energetic freedom of the constitutional rights of the colonies, and of the oppressive measures of Parliament; but their first resolves were more moderate, than perhaps England herself had expected. An invitation to a general agreement against all trade with Great Britain was the only active step they allowed themselves; and after all what the Parliament had done, this step was of little importance. How far they were remote, even then, from a total separation, and how much the conduct of the colonies deserved the name of a lawful defense, may be learned from the following conclusion of the remarkable address, which this congress immediately before separating, sent to the king.

> We ask only for peace, liberty and security. We wish no diminution of royal prerogatives, we demand *no new rights*. From the magnanimity and justice of your majesty, and the Parliament, we promise ourselves the redress of our grievances; firmly convinced, that when once the causes of our present complaints are removed, our future conduct will not be undeserving of the milder treatment, to which we were in better days accustomed. We call that Being, who tries the inmost heart, to witness, that no other motive, than the fear of the destruction, which threatens us, has had any influence upon our resolutions. We therefore entreat your majesty as the loving father of all your people, bound to you by the ties of blood, by laws, affection, and fidelity, not to permit, in the uncertain expectation of a result, which never can compensate for the wretchedness by which it must be attained, any further violation of those sacred ties. So, may your majesty in a long and glorious reign, enjoy every earthly bliss, and this bliss, and your undiminished authority descend upon your heirs and their heirs, till time shall be no more.

The American agents in London, Bollan, Franklin and Lee, petitioned to be heard in support of this address, at the bar of the Parliament. Their request was rejected.

Soon after, this cruel act, which deprived the colonies of all navigation, and even of the fishery, obtained the force of law; and the very moment, when this harsh law was passed, was chosen to make the only proposal of conciliation, which the Parliament had ever offered. According to this proposal, which is known by the name of Lord North's Conciliatory Plan, every colony, whose representatives would engage to deliver their proportional contribution to the exigencies of the empire, and raise besides the costs of their internal administration, *provided* their offers should be approved by the king and Parliament, was to be secured in the exemption from all further taxation. Not to mention that the only object of this plan notoriously was to divide the colonies, that it was offered them by an armed hand, that the *suspicious proviso* made the favorable consequences of its acceptance extremely doubtful, it properly decided the true point of contest, in a manner wholly contradictory to the principles of the Americans. The Parliament renounced a right which notoriously did not belong to them. But they renounced it, only to exercise, once for all, what they had wished to exercise by piece-meal. The injustice and inconsistency of this proposal could not for a moment escape the notice of the colonies. The second general congress, which assembled on the 10th of May, 1775,3- rejected it upon grounds, the force of which must be felt by every impartial mind. "Should we accede," say they, in their answer to this proposal...

> ...we should expressly declare a wish to purchase the favor of Parliament, without knowing at what price it would be set. We hold it superfluous to extort from us, by violence or threats a proportional contribution, to meet the general exigencies of the state, since all the world knows, and the Parliament must themselves acknowledge, that

whenever thereto required, in a constitutional manner, we have always richly contributed. It is unjust to require permanent contributions of the colonies, so long as Great Britain possesses the monopoly of their trade; this monopoly is, in itself, the heaviest of all contributions. It is unjust to wish to tax us doubly. If we must contribute in like proportion with the other parts of the empire, allow us, like them too, a free trade with all the world.

These unanswerable arguments were at an immeasurable distance from the language of insolent rebellion.

When, finally, the congress resolved upon the general arming of the country, *defense* was still their single, and exclusive object. The constitution had been long since, without their fault, torn to pieces; they might have proclaimed immediately a new one upon its ruins; but they appealed to arms, to maintain the same constitution, of which the colonies had been, with so much violence, deprived.

The surest proof of this glorious moderation was, that they themselves, after the actual breaking out of hostilities, and when a great part of the inhabitants of America, urged for more energetic measures, did not omit another attempt by petitions and remonstrances, to attain the end of their wishes. In the midst of the most vigorous preparations for a desperate defense, they resolved, in the month of July, 1775,[20] another address to the king, to which was given the inviting and significant name of the *olive branch*. Even in this last address, we read with astonishment, among other things, as follows:

> Devoted to the person, the family, and the government of your majesty, with all the attachment, which only principle and feeling can inspire, connected with Great Britain, by the strongest ties that can unite human societies together, deeply afflicted at every event that may weaken this connection, we most solemnly assure your majesty, that

we wish *nothing more ardently than the restoration of the former harmony* between England and the colonies, and a new union, founded upon a lasting basis, capable of propagating that blessed harmony to the latest generations, and transmit to a grateful posterity your majesty's name, surrounded with that immortal glory which was in every age bestowed upon the saviors of the people. We protest to your majesty, that notwithstanding all our sufferings in this unhappy contest, the hearts of your faithful colonists are far from wishing a reconciliation upon conditions, which could be inconsistent with the dignity, or the welfare of the state from which they sprung, and which they love with filial tenderness. If the grievances, which now bow us down with inexpressible pain to the ground, could in any manner be removed, your majesty will at all times find your faithful subjects in America, willing and ready, with their lives and fortunes, to maintain, preserve, and defend the rights and interests of their sovereign, and of their mother country.

This was the address, which Mr. Penn, on the 1st of September, 1775, delivered to the earl of Dartmouth, upon which, some days after, he was informed, *that no answer could be given.* It was not until after this last attempt had proved fruitless, after an unmerciful statute had outlawed American ships, and the levying of foreign troops left them only the choice between the dissolution of their constitution, with unconditional submission, and the same dissolution with the free choice of a new one, that the congress passed the resolve, which reason and necessity prescribed, and declared the colonies independent, because independence was a smaller evil than dependence upon arbitrary will; and their painfully maintained, and painfully defended dependence upon the old laws, was lost forever.

The Revolution of America was, therefore, in every sense of the word, a Revolution of necessity: England, alone, had by violence effected it: America had contended ten years long, not against England, but against the Revolution: America sought not a revolution; she yielded to it, compelled by necessity, not because she wished to extort a better condition than she had before enjoyed, but because she wished to avert a worse one, prepared for her.

Exactly the contrary of all this, was the case in France. The French Revolution was *offensive* in its origin, offensive in its progress, offensive in its whole compass, and in every single characteristic moment of its existence. As the American Revolution had exhibited a model of moderation in defense, so the French one displayed an unparalleled example of violence and inexorable fury in attack. As the former had always kept the vigor of its defensive measures in rigorous proportion to the exigency, so the latter, from the weakness of the resistance made against it, became more and more violent and terrible, the more cause it had to grow milder.

Could the destroyers of a throne, could the teachers and heroes of a revolutionary age, themselves have formed the character of a prince, under whom they would begin their dreadful experiment, they never could have succeeded better, than in that, which a cruel destiny delivered into their hands. Lewis the 16th promoted the Revolution by all the good, and by all the weak sides of his character. 33 He was certainly not equal to the circumstances, under which he had to act, and to the dangers, which he was to overcome; but what rendered his want of energy truly fatal, were his virtues. Had he been less honorable, less benevolent, less humane, less conscientious, perhaps he might yet have saved the monarchy. The unhappy certainty that it was impossible for him, so much as for a moment, to be a tyrant, made him and the state the victims of the most shameful and most revolting tyranny that the world had ever seen. His noble readiness to encourage everything, which assumed the name of reform, drew him into the first false steps, which shook his throne. His horror of violence tore the scepter from his benevolent hands. His integrity was the best ally of those, who plunged France and him into the precipice.

He looked with satisfaction towards that assembly of the states, whose effects had in the council of the wicked been long prepared. They rewarded him by the decrees, which excluded him from the government of the kingdom. He would not suffer his troops to use force against the first insurgents. They rewarded him by the general insurrection of the capital and of all the provinces. He endeavored, even after having lost all his power, and tasted the bitterest afflictions, such as a dethroned monarch only can know, still to turn the evil to good. They improved this insurmountable royal temper, this pure and real civism, to be guilty with less interruption, while he continued to hope; and to crush him with the load of their present crimes, while he looked forward to a better futurity.

It may boldly be maintained almost everything that has been said of the resistance of the court and of the great, of their conspiracies, of their cabals against the Revolution, was merely a wretched fable. That the injured, the oppressed, the plundered could be no friends to their oppressors and plunderers is self-evident; as far as mere hatred is resistance, there was an enormous mass of resistance against the Revolution; the leaders had themselves created these internal, these secret hostilities, of which they so often complained. They must have extirpated human nature herself to secure to themselves forgiveness, or a disposition to favor their cruel operations. But, throughout their whole career, they met with no active resistance, and the only circumstance, which could spread a varnish of credibility over their incessant fictions of plots, counter-revolutions, &c. was, that they *deserved* all, that they pretended to suffer.

If we follow this Revolution through all its periods, we shall find that the strongest motive for effecting any greater usurpation, for maintaining any greater injustice, for committing any greater crime, constantly was, that a smaller one had immediately before succeeded. The single motive for using persecutions, was, that the victims had already suffered others. This was the character of the French Revolution, in wholesale and in retail. The sufferers were punishable, merely because they had suffered; in this bitterest of all offensive wars, they seemed so cautiously to shun everything that made a show of resistance, that they sooner forgave a struggling, than a defenseless, enemy.

The relics of the old constitution were not so much boundaries to the omnipotent desolating power of the Revolution, as land-marks, designating its victorious progress. The constitution, of 1791, was only a short and voluntary pause; a sort of resting point, at which nobody meant long to wait. The second national assembly did not make a pass, no, not one, which was not an attack upon some ruin or other of the monarchy. The establishment of the republic did not satisfy its authors. The execution of the king scarcely appeased the ravenousness of his butchers, for a single instant. In the year 1793 the thirst for destruction had gone so far, that it was at a loss for an object. The well-known saying, that Robespierre meant to reduce the population of France by one half, had its foundation in the lively sense of the impossibility of satisfying the hitherto insatiate revolution, with anything less, than such a hecatomb.

When there was nothing more left in the country to attack, the offensive frenzy turned itself against the neighboring states, and finally declared war in solemn decrees against all civil society. It was certainly not the want of will in those, who then conducted this war, if Europe preserved anything, besides "bread and iron." Fortunately, no strength was great enough long to support such a will. The unavoidable exhaustion of the assailants, and not the power or the merit of the resistance made, saved society; and, finally, brought the workshops themselves, where the weapons for its destruction were forged, within its beneficent bonds again.

As the American Revolution was a defensive revolution, it was of course finished, at the moment, when it had overcome the attack, by which it had been occasioned. The French Revolution, true to the character of a most violent offensive revolution, could not but proceed so long as there remained objects for it to attack, and it retained strength for the assault.

3. The American Revolution, at every stage of its duration, had a fixed and definite object, and moved within definite limits, and by a definite direction towards this object. The French Revolution never had a definite object; and, in a thousand various directions, continually crossing each other, ran through the unbounded space of a fantastic arbitrary will, and of a bottomless anarchy.

It lay in the very nature of a defensive revolution, like that of America, to proceed from definite objects, and to pursue definite ends. The peculiar situation, and the peculiar character of the North Americans confirmed and secured this moderate and beneficent quality to the progress of their Revolution.

In the course of it, two principal periods may be observed; *that*, from the first breaking out of the contests in 1765, until the Declaration of Independence in 1776, and *that*, from this Declaration, until the peace with England.

In the first period, the single towns and provinces, and afterwards the members of the general congress, had for their declared and sole object the salvation of their constitution, and of their rights and liberties, as they then stood, from the oppressive usurpations of the British Parliament. And I think I have clearly shown, in the former sections of this essay, that every step they took, during that critical period was calculated for preservation, not for conquest, for resistance against innovations, not for ardor after them; for de-fence, not for attack.

In the second period, indeed, a new object came in the place of that, which they had until then pursued: the British Parliament had compelled the congress to proclaim the independence of the colonies; but, even this decisive measure by no means threw America into the precipice of lawlessness, into the horrible gulf of an unmeasurable interregnum, or into the slippery career of wild and chimerical theories—The machine of government was, and remained, completely organized: the Revolution had taken from the king his negative upon legislative acts, almost the only essential prerogative, which as sovereign of the colonies he immediately exercised: but every province took care that this important function should be performed by another authority, distinct from the legislature, and Georgia and Pennsylvania, were the only ones, which entrusted the legislative powers to an undivided senate. The royal governors, who till then had stood at the head of the executive power, were replaced by others, chosen by the provinces themselves; and as the former governors, owing to their great distance from the mother country, had always held powers in the highest degree discretionary and independent, this alteration could not be much felt. The great and immediate exigencies of social life, the local administration, the police, and course of judicial proceeding were continued as before. Nothing but the loose tie, which had connected America with England, was broken; none of the internal relations were discomposed; all the laws remained in force; the condition of persons and of property suffered no other revolution, than that which was necessarily brought with it! "The people," says that very well-informed American historian Dr. Ramsay, "scarcely perceived that an alteration in their political constitution had taken place."

As the founders and conductors of the American Revolution, from the beginning, knew exactly how far they were to go, and where they must stop; as the new existence of their country, the constitutions of the several provinces, and even the organization of the federal government, at least in its principles was definitely prescribed to them; as their purpose was in no sort to create, but only to preserve, not to erect a new building, but to free the old one from an external, burdensome, straitening scaffolding, and as it never occurred to them, in the rigorous sense of the word, to *reform*, even their own country, much less the whole world, they escaped the most dangerous of all the rocks, which in our times threaten the founders of any great revolution, the deadly passion for making political experiments with abstract theories, and untried systems. It is of the utmost importance, in judging the American Revolution, never to lose sight of this point, and by so much the more important, as certain expressions in the early resolves of congress, the maxims of single writers, but especially the frequent appeals of the first leaders of the French Revolution to the example of their predecessors in America, have encouraged, and spread abroad the opinion that these, in truth, opened the wide field of revolutionary speculations, and of systematic anarchy. True it is, that the Declaration of Independence published by the congress, in the name of the colonies, is proceeded by an introduction, in which the *natural* and *unalienable* rights of mankind are considered as the foundation of all government; that after this assertion, so indefinite, and so exposed to the greatest misconstructions, follow certain principles, no less indefinite, no less liable to be abused, from which an inference might be drawn of the unlimited right of the people to change their form of government, and what in the new revolutionary language, is called their *sovereignty*. It is likewise true, that most of the constitutions of the United States, are preceded by those idle *Declaration of Rights*, so dangerous in their application, from which so much misery has at a later period been derived upon France, and the whole civilized world. Much, however, as it were to be wished, that the legislators of America had disdained this empty pomp of words, that they had exclusively confined themselves within the clear and lawful motives of their resistance; a resistance at first constitutional, and afterwards necessary, and within the limits of their incontrovertible rights, yet it cannot escape the observation of those, who attentively study the history of their Revolution, that they allowed to these speculative ideas, no visible influence upon their practical measures and resolves—They erroneously believed them necessary to justify their first steps;[21] but here the dominion of empty speculation, was forever abandoned. Never, in the whole course of the American Revolution, were the *rights of man*, appealed to, for the destruction of the *rights of a citizen*; never was the sovereignty of the people used as a pretext to undermine the respect, due to the laws, or the foundations of social security; no example was ever seen of an individual, or a whole class of individuals, or even the representatives of this, or that single state, who recurred to the Declaration of Rights, to escape from positive obligation, or to renounce obedience to the common sovereign; finally, never did it enter the head of any legislator, or statesman in America, to combat the lawfulness of foreign constitutions, and to set up the American Revolution, as a new epoch in the general relations of civil society.

What was here and there occasionally said by single writers, must carefully be distinguished from the principles and way of thinking of those Americans, who were acknowledged and revered as examples and authorities, but especially from those, who took an active part in the new government. There certainly was in America, a Thomas Paine; and I will not deny but that his celebrated work had influence among certain classes of people, and so far, contributed to promote the Revolution.[22] But to judge of the spirit and principles of the American Revolution by this work, would be as unjust, as to confound the efficaciously active heads in the English Revolution, of 1688, with the authors of some popular lampoon against the house of Stewart; or the opposition of lord Chatham, with that of Mr. Wilkes. When Paine's work appeared, in the year 1776, the American Revolution had long since assumed its whole form and consistence, and the principles, which will forever characterize it stood firm. In no public resolve, in no public debate, in no state paper of congress, is the most distant expression to be found, which discovers either a formal, or a tacit approbation of a systematical revolutionary policy. And what a contrast between the wild, extravagant, rhapsodical declamation of a Paine, and the mild, moderate, and considerate tone in the speeches and letters of a Washington.

The preciseness of objects, the uniformity of means, and the moderation of principles, which distinguished the American Revolution through all its periods, gave likewise to the war, which was carried on for its establishment and completion, a precise and definite, and, therefore, a less formidable character. With this war indeed, the whole train of evils, which usually attend upon war in general, and especially upon civil war, were connected. But as it had only one object, and that was clearly known, and confined within narrow bounds, its possible results, its possible consequences, and its possible duration, could in every case be calculated. America had either to maintain or to give up her independence; in this single alternative was included the whole fate of the contest; and whatever consequence either event might operate upon a distant futurity, neither the victory of the British Parliament, nor that (which very early became more probable) of the American congress, could discompose the balance of Europe, or threaten its peace. The governments of our hemisphere could, with all the tranquility of a perfect neutrality, look forward to the issue of a remote contest, which, without further danger to their external and internal political relations, opened an advantageous prospect to the European commerce. The congress might even form an alliance with one of the greatest European monarchies; for as they only wished to maintain clear and definite rights, as they owed their existence to a revolution, which was forced upon the colonies by external violence, as they had at no time, and in no way, so much as called in question, much less attacked, the lawfulness of other constitutions, and as they had declared war, not against monarchical principles, but only against the oppressive measures of the British ministry, there was, *in itself*, nothing unnatural, nothing revolting, nothing plainly irreconcilable with the maxims of the law of nations, and the laws of self-preservation, in the alliance, which France contracted with them.[23]

The peace, which concluded the American war, secured that existence independent of England, to the new federal republic, for which she had alone and exclusively contended, and immediately after, this republic entered into those peaceable and beneficent relations with all other states, and even with England herself, which the common wants, and the common laws of nations have founded between civilized states. It is true; the American Revolution had in latter times a decisive influence upon the great devastations under which Europe groans to this hour; 4£ but it would be the highest injustice not to acknowledge that this influence was only accidental. In the origin of that Revolution there was nothing that could justify another, or even revolutions in general; no state, other than one, in which all the extraordinary circumstances concurring in the case of the colonies, should again concur, could consider the conduct observed by these, as legitimating a similar conduct, and adopt the principles upon which they proceeded. The precision and lawfulness of their object refused every application of these principles to revolutions, which could not exhibit an object equally definite, and a right equally clear, to the pursuit of that object. The wise moderation, which the leaders of the American Revolution introduced into all their declarations, and into every step they took, their glorious abhorrence of every extravagance, even of those proceeding from the most pardonable enthusiasm, the constant distance at which they kept from everything that may be called proselyting and propagandism—all these happy characteristics of their undertaking must in a legal point of view forever secure humanity against all evil consequences of this Revolution; whose only traces remaining, should be in the growing prosperity of a great people, spread over extensive and fertile regions, and above all in the wholesome lesson it gave to the powers of the earth against every attack upon the rights and constitutions of states, from ambition, or a spirit of innovation. The harshest injustice alone could impute to the Americans, what the ill-understood and misused example of their Revolution has produced of evil in latter times; it was the work of an hostile demon, who seems to have condemned the close of the eighteenth century, to see the buds of destruction shoot from the most beneficent events, and the most poisonous fruits from the blossoms of its fairest hopes.

The contrast between the French and American Revolutions, when you compare them with each other in respect to their *objects* is no less striking than that which has resulted from the comparison of their *origin* and *progress*. As the utmost precision of object, and consequently of principles and of means, distinguished the American Revolution through its whole duration, so the utmost want of precision in the object, and consequently a perpetual mutability in the choice of the means and in the modification of principles has been one of the most stubborn, one of the most essential, and certainly one of the most terrible characteristics of the French Revolution. Its history was nothing but a long series of uninterrupted developments of this extraordinary phenomenon; single and unexampled in its whole compass as this circumstance may be, it will not much astonish the man, who shall reflect upon its origin, and its nature. For so soon as in a great undertaking, a step is taken wholly out of the boundaries of definite rights, and everything is declared lawful, which imaginary necessity, or unbridled passion inspires, so soon is the immeasurable field of arbitrary will entered upon; and a revolution, which has no other principle than to attack the existing constitution, must necessarily proceed to the last extremities of imagination and of criminal guilt.

When, by the impotence and the faults of the government, and by the success which crowned the hardiness of its first antagonists, the old constitution of France was dissolved, all those who took an interest in favor of the Revolution (and their number was infinitely great, precisely because no one knew exactly what he meant by a revolution) concurred, that an essential and wide spreading alteration must be effected in the whole political constitution of the state. But how far this alteration should extend, how far the old order of things should be preserved, and how the new one should be organized, with regard to all this, no two persons of the legions, who thought themselves called to public activity, were agreed. If we confine ourselves merely to the opinions of those, who in this interval of unbounded anarchy, publicly wrote, or spoke, we shall soon be convinced, that there were then in France, not three, or four, or ten, but thousands of political sects and parties. The impossibility of taking notice of so many individual variations, distinctions, sub-distinctions, and shades of every kind, compelled the contemporaries, and especially those immediately interested in the great spectacle, to class the infinite mass of opinions under certain known principal titles, and thus erase the names of *pure royalists*, of whole and half *monarchists*, of *feuillants*, of *jacobins*, of every degree, &c. Each of these parties, however, could have exhibited almost as many subordinate parties as it contained members.

In this number of political systems, some were built upon a limited monarchy, in the British sense of the word, others upon a thousand-fold new modification of a constitution, monarchical only in name; some wished from the beginning, to treat the Revolution merely as a passage to the utter abolition of the monarchy. These pronounced sentence of death upon all the privileges of the higher orders; others wished to leave them the prerogatives of rank. One was for reforming the constitution of the churches; another for extirpating religion: one would have shown mercy in this general overthrow, at least to the rights of property; another was for passing all positive right, under the sickle of equality. The constitution of 1791, was a desperate and impotent attempt to reconcile together, by a sort of general capitulation, all these contending theories, and the infinitely multiplied motives of interest, of ambition, and of vanity, connected with them; this attempt of course failed, for in the absolute and total indefiniteness, and I might add, the impossibility of ascertaining the last object of the Revolution, every individual in France felt but too well, that he had as much right to maintain his private opinion, and to carry through his private purposes, as the members of a committee had to establish theirs; it was, besides, more than doubtful, whether, even the immediate authors of this impracticable constitution, seriously considered it as a last result.

Under the shelter of the inexpressible confusion, in which the storm of these first debates involved the whole country, arose, at first, more timid, but from the last months of the year 1791, growing constantly bolder, and more powerful, the only consistent party; that which had always been of opinion, that it was folly to prescribe to the French Revolution, any bounds whatsoever. This party had, indeed, like all the rest, a multitude of subdivisions, and of systems peculiarly modified, and often at violent strife with each other; but all who declared themselves for it, concurred in the great and decisive point of view, that the Revolution was to be considered, not as a local transaction, but as one of those, which give a new form to civil society, and which must draw all mankind within its vortex. For the ambition, or for the enthusiasm of this insatiable party, the theatre, which France offered to their thirst for destruction, was too small; they wished to tear up the world from its poles, and commence a new era for the whole human race. 5- That this was their purpose, from the very breaking out, and even before the breaking out of the French Revolution, we need not learn from proselyting tales and imaginary cabals of the illuminati; the writings in which they have unfolded their principles in plain terms, have proved it beyond all contradiction.

To draw nearer the execution of so gigantic a plan, they had first of all to destroy the last trace of a monarchical form of government in France. It would be hard to maintain, that, after all what had happened since 1789, they had not nearly about the same right to found a republic, as the monarchists, so called, had to introduce a royal democracy. The only thing which seemed against them, in point of right, was the oath which, in common with all the rest, they had taken, to support the constitution of 1791. But, after so many bands had been torn, none but weak heads could flatter themselves, that an empty form would arrest the torrent in its course. At the very time, while, with the cry of "The constitution or death!" they hushed a few credulous souls to repose, they were working with restless activity the mine, which in one instant was to blow up the whole fabric.

But, precisely at this great and important moment, the absolute indefinitude of object, that inextinguishable character of the French Revolution, discovered itself in a new and terrible light. The republic had been proclaimed; but this republic was a word without definite meaning, which everyone believed he might explain, according to his inclinations, and according to the fantastic whims, which he called his principles. There were just as many republican systems contending for the mastery, as there had been monarchical parties. France was drenched in blood, to decide the great question, whether Brissot, or Marat, the federalists, or the unitists, the Girondists, or the mountaineers, the Dantonians, or the Hebertists, should prescribe a republican constitution. Force alone could determine the issue of this horrible contest; and the victory must necessarily remain to the most resolute. After having torn, for nearly a year, the inmost bowels of their country, without being able to agree upon the form of their republic, a daring faction, at length, fell upon the strange expedient of settling and organizing the Revolutionary state itself, as a provisional government, and, under the name of a revolutionary government, brought into play what was called the system of terror; a monstrous and unexampled monument of human error and human frenzy, which in the eyes of posterity will almost degrade the history of our times to a fable. A less cruel faction overthrew and murdered the inventors of this gigantic wickedness; not long afterwards, another devised a new code of anarchy, which was called the constitution of the third year. it is well known, by what an uninterrupted series of revolutions, and counter-revolutions, this constitution was likewise conducted to the unavoidable catastrophe of its destruction.

Just at the period, when the republican party obtained possession of the supreme power, the bloody contest broke out between them and the greatest part of the European states. They had denounced the destruction of all governments; they had declared, that between their Revolution and those who rejected it, no further intercourse could exist; they had solemnly absolved all subjects from obedience to their governments. The Revolution prepared against Europe, and Europe against the Revolution, a war, with which only the most dreadful religious wars, that ever scourged the world, can be compared. On the side of the coalesced powers, the proper object of this war could not be doubtful; and if, unfortunately, it often was, at least it ought never to have been so. But, on the side of France, it was always as indefinite as the object of the Revolution itself. Some, as for instance, Robespierre, wished for the present, only to maintain the right of turning their own country into a butchery, with impunity, and to reduce by one half the number of its inhabitants; others had projected extensive plans of conquest, and wished to realize for the French republic, all the dreams, which the ambition of Lewis the XIVth, had formerly inspired; others yet had sworn never to lay down their arms, until they should have led the principles of the Revolution in triumph over the whole civilized world, or *have planted, at least*, the tree of liberty, from Lisbon to the frozen sea, and to the Dardanelles.

This war has now, with short and local intervals of insecure and treacherous peace, already desolated the earth eight years long; it has, undoubtedly, for some time past, lost much of its extent, and very much of its original character, and has now nearly declined to a common war; yet when and how it will end, is still a problem, which puts all human penetration to the blush. The fate of the French revolution is, in a great measure, connected with the fate of this war; but its last result depends, besides, upon an infinity of other combinations. There has, perhaps, never yet been a man, who could even imagine, with any clearness, what this result will be. When one of the great masses of the physical world is suddenly started from its quiet center of gravitation, and hurled with a prodigious impetus into the empty space of air, the point at which it will stop is much harder to conceive, than the continuance of its motion. And, in truth, after the serious question, "Who could have a right to begin such a revolution?" has remained unanswered, nothing is more difficult than to answer that, which is equally serious: to whom belongs the right of ending it?

4. The American revolution had a mass of resistance, comparatively much smaller to combat, and, therefore, could form and consolidate itself in a manner comparatively much easier, and more simple: the French revolution challenged almost every human feeling, and every human passion, to the most vehement resistance, and could therefore only force its way by violence and crimes.

The American colonies had already, before their revolution, attained a high degree of stability; and the supremacy of the British government in America, was the relation, not so much of an immediate sovereign, as of a superior protector. Hence, the American revolution had more the appearance of a foreign, than of a civil war.

A common feeling of the uprightness of their cause, and a common interest in its issue must necessarily have animated a great and overpowering majority of the inhabitants of North America. The royal governors, the persons more immediately connected with them, and the inconsiderable number of royal troops constituted the only permanent and great opposition party. If a certain number of independent citizens, from principle, or from inclination took the side of the ministry, they were however much too weak to become dangerous to the rest; and their impotence itself protected them against the hatred and intolerance of their countrymen.

There were in the interior of the colonies no sort of zeal or personal prerogatives, and no other distinction of ranks, than what proceeded from the exercise of public functions. Property owing to the novelty of civil society in the country, was much more equally distributed than can be the case in old countries, and the relations between the wealthy and the laboring classes were more simple and therefore more beneficent. As the Revolution altered little in the internal organization of the colonies, as it only dissolved an external connection, which the Americans must always have considered rather as a burden, than an advantage; there was nobody, except the few, who took a share in the administration at the head of the country, who was immediately and essentially interested in the preservation of the ancient form. What this form contained of good and useful remained untouched; the Revolution only removed that in which it had been oppressive.

How infinitely different was in this point of view the situation of France! If the French revolution had been content merely to destroy with violent hands the old Constitution, without making any attack upon the rights and possessions of private persons, it would, however, have been contrary to the interest of a numerous, and in every respect important class of people, who by the sudden dissolution of the old form of Government, having lost their offices, their incomes, their estimation and their whole civil existence, would of themselves have formed a powerful opposition. But, when in its further progress, it no longer spared any private right whatsoever, when it declared all political prerogatives to be usurpations, deprived the nobility not only of their real privileges, but likewise of their rank and title, robbed the clergy of their possessions, of their influence, and even of their external dignity; by arbitrary laws took from the holders of estates half their revenues; by incessant breaches of the rights of property, converted property itself into an uncertain, equivocal, narrowly straitened enjoyment, by recognizing publicly principles of the most dangerous tendency, held the sword hovering over the head of every one, who had anything to lose, and aggravated the essential wretchedness, which it everywhere spread by the ridicule and contempt it shed over everything that bore the name of possessions, or privileges—then truly it could not fail to accumulate against itself a mass of resistance, which was not to be subdued by ordinary means.

Should the friends of the French revolution declare this important circumstance to be merely accidental; should they impute solely to the good fortune of the American nation, that they found no domestic impediments in the way to their new constitution; and to the ill fortune of the French, that they had to struggle with so many obstinate antagonists; should they consider the former case only as enviable, and the latter only as deserving compassion, yet will the impartial observer, never forget how much merit there was involved in that good, and how much guilt in this ill fortune. The Americans were wise enough to circumscribe themselves within the bounds, which right, on one side, and the nature of things, on the other, had drawn round them. The French in their giddiness no longer acknowledged the prescriptions of the clearest right, nor the prescriptions of nature. They were so proud as to think they could bend impossibility itself, under the arm of their violence,— and so daring that they thought the clearest right must yield to the maxims of their arbitrary will. The resistance of which they complained, was with perfect certainty to be foreseen; it lay in the unalterable laws of human feelings, and human passions; it was just, it was necessary; it was impossible to believe that it would not take place. Those, who had called it forth by the most cruel injuries, did not fail to be sure to declare it punishable, and did punish thousands, whose only crime consisted in refusing to rejoice at their own ruin. But this double injustice prepared a new resistance, which could be overcome only by new acts of violence. Thus at last, in the barbarous law book of the Revolution, suffering itself was made an unpardonable offence; the fear of a just reaction drove the authors of these oppressions to measures of still deepening cruelty against the victims of their first crimes; and the presumption of the natural and inevitable hatred, which these crimes must everywhere rouse against them, was a sufficient ground to them to treat as an offender deserving death, every man, who did not immediately and actively associate with them.

Although the American revolution never involved itself in this horrible labyrinth, where voluntary iniquities can only be covered by necessary misdeeds, and where every earlier crime became the only justification of an hundred later ones; yet did it not altogether escape the misfortune, which seems inseparable from all sudden and violent changes in the civil and political relations of society. The smallness of the resistance it met with, and the moderation of those who conducted it, preserved it from a multitude of cruel, desperate, and dishonorable measures, which have sullied other revolutions; but its warmest friends will not venture to maintain that it was wholly exempt from injustice and violence. The bitterness against the English government, often degenerated into a spirit of persecution, and involved those, who were suspected of a punishable indifference, or of secret connivance, in the sentence of proscription pronounced against tyranny. The hatred between the friends of independence, and the partisans of the ministry, the Whigs and the Tories, as they were distinguished by names taken from old English parties, broke out, especially amidst the dangers of the war, sometimes in violent scenes, which tore to pieces the internal harmony of neighborhoods, and sometimes even of families. The reciprocal cruelties, which from time to time were practiced upon prisoners, called to mind the peculiar character, which had never wholly abandoned a civil war. The rights of property likewise were often violated by single communities and single states, and, in some few instances, with the co-operation of the supreme authority. The history of the descendants, of the great and benevolent Penn, driven from the paradise, which he had created, and compelled, like other loyalists, to take refuge in the generosity and magnanimity of England, is no honorable page in the annals of North America.

But what are all these single instances of injustice and oppression, compared with the universal flood of misery and ruin, which the French revolution let loose upon France, and all the neighboring countries. If, even in America, private hatred, or local circumstances, threatened property or personal security; if here and there even the public authorities became the instruments of injustice, of revenge, and of a persecuting spirit, yet did the poison never flow into every vein of the social body; never, as in France, was the contempt of all rights, and of the very simplest precepts of humanity, made the general maxim of legislation, and the unqualified prescription of systematic tyranny. If in America, the confusion of the moment, the impulse of necessity, or the eruption of the passions, sometimes inflicted misfortune upon innocence, never at least, never as in France, did reason herself, abused, desecrated reason, ascend the theatre of misery, solemnly to justify, by cold blooded, criminal appeals to principles and duties, these revolutionary confusions; and if in America, single families and districts, felt the heavy hand of the Revolution and of war, never at least, as in France, were confiscations, banishments, imprisonments, and death, decreed in a mass.

When the American revolution was concluded, the country proceeded with rapid steps to a new, a happy, and a flourishing constitution. Not but that the Revolution had left behind it many great and essential ravages: the ties of public order, had, in a long and bloody contest, been on all sides more or less relaxed; peaceful industry had suffered many a violent interruption; the relations of property, the culture of the soil, the internal and foreign trade, the public and private credit, had all considerably suffered by the Revolutionary storms, by the insecurity of the external relations, and especially by the devastations of paper money.[24] Even the morals and the character of the people, had been essentially, and not in every respect advantageously affected by the Revolution. Although we can draw no conclusion from this circumstance with regard to futurity, yet history must remark with attention, and preserve with care, the confession, which comes from the pen of a calm and impartial witness, the best of all the writers upon the American revolution hitherto (Ramsay): "That by this Revolution, the political, military, and literary talents of the people of the United States, were improved, but their moral qualities were deteriorated. "

A picture of the condition in which the Revolution has left France, is by far too great, too complicated, and too formidable a subject to be touched upon even transiently here. The idea itself of a final result from such a revolution as this, must still be in some sort an indefinite, and perhaps a hazarded idea. Thus much, however, may be asserted with confidence, that between the results of the American and those of the French revolution, no sort of comparison can so much as be conceived.

I might have continued the above parallel through many other respects, and perhaps into single points of detail. I believe, however, that the four principal points of view in which I have treated it, with regard to the lawfulness of the origin, character of the conduct, quality of the object, and compass of resistance, sufficiently answer the purpose, I proposed to myself, and it appears, at least to me, evident enough, that every parallel between these two revolutions, will serve much more to display the contrast, than the resemblance between them.

THE END

CITED IN TEXT

Reference Notes

Supporting Evidence

It should be noted that the numbering of endnote is sequential throughout the entire work.

1 Clinton Rossiter, *Seedtime of the Republic: The Origin of the American Tradition of Political Liberty* (New York: Harcourt, Brace, 1953), 149-312.

2 Donald S. Lutz, *The Origin of American Constitutionalism* (Baton Rouge: Louisiana State University Press, 1988), 140.

3 Lutz, *Origin of American Constitutionalism*, 139-147. Also see Charles S. Hyneman and Donald S. Lutz, *American Political Writing During the Founding Era, 1760-1805*, 2 vols. (Indianapolis: Liberty Press, 1983).

4 Donald Lutz, "The Relative Influence of European Writers on Late Eighteenth-Century American Political Thought," *American Political Science Review* 189 (1984): 189-97.

5 John Quincy Adams, *Writings of John Quincy Adams* (New York, NY: Greenwood Press, 1968), 2:463-64.

6   Benjamin Franklin and Jared Sparks, *The Works of Benjamin Franklin: Containing Several Political and Historical Tracts Not Included in Any Former Edition and Many Letters Official and Private, Not Hitherto Published: With Notes and a Life of the Author*, 10 vols. (Boston: Hilliard, Gray, and Company, 1836-1840), 10:281-82.

7   Elias Boudinot, *The Age of Revelation, or, the Age of Reason Shewn to Be an Age of Infidelity* (Philadelphia: Asbury Dickins, 1801).

8   "John Adams to Zabdiel Adams, 21 June 1776," Founders Online, National Archives, May 16, 2020; https://founders.archives.gov/documents/Adams/04-02-02-0011.

9   Original orthography updated. *The Papers of Thomas Jefferson, vol. 6, Retirement Series, 11 March to 27 November 1813* (Princeton: Princeton University Press, 2009), 236-39.

10   John Quincy Adams, *An Address, Delivered at the Request of the Committee of Arrangements for Celebrating the Anniversary of Independence : At the City of Washington on the Fourth of July 1821, Upon the Occasion of Reading the Declaration of Independence* (Cambridge, [MA]: University Press by Hilliard and Metcalf, 1821), 28-29.

11   "Friedrich Von Gentz," Wikipedia, May 16, 2020; https://en.wikipedia.org/wiki/Friedrich_von_Gentz.

12   Adams, *Writings of John Quincy Adams*, 2:520.

13   [**This note and following are believed to be provided by the author, Friedrich Gentz**] Thus, for example, among all the statesmen and literati, who spoke or wrote, either for or against the American Revolution, there were only two, who even then foresaw that the loss of the colonies would be no misfortune for England: The one, Adam Smith, was at that time

little read, and, perhaps, little understood; the other, Dean Tucker, was held and eccentric visionary.

14 So long as the colonists had found a paramount advantage in the *culture of the land*, they would probably have borne their dependence. But when the critical period had arrived, when in the natural progress of society, a considerable part of the capitals would have been employed in *manufactures*, the English monopoly would have become insupportable.

15 Lord North formally declared in Parliament, that after what had happened, and entire repeal of all the new taxes could not take place, until America should be brought to the feet of Great Britain.

16 This great man, who, faithful to the principles of ancient policy, and animated with the most unbounded zeal for the glory and welfare of his country, which under his administration had reached the zenith of her greatness, considered the separation of the colonies from England, as the greatest of evils, said among other things, in a most impressive speech, with which on the 20th of January, 1775, he introduced the motion for withdrawing the troops from Boston. "I announce it to you now, my Lords, we shall one day be *compelled* to repeal these oppressive regulations, the *must* be repealed; you yourselves will retract them. I pledge myself for it; I stake my reputation upon it; I am content to pass for a blockhead, if they are not retracted."

It is furthermore very remarkable, that the disapprobation of the measures against America, was not confined to the then *opposition parties*, but was equally shown by several of the principal ministers. The Duke of Grafton, who from 1766 to 1770, was the first Lord of the Treasury, and afterwards, from 1771 to 1775, keeper of the seals, had at all times declared himself against the prevailing system; the same sentiments were ascribed to the Earl of Dartmouth, Secretary of State for America; Lord North himself, who from 1770, was considered as First Minister, is said to have manifested often in the deliberations of the Cabinet, different principles from those he afterwards supported in Parliament. But nothing can be more surprising, than that in one of the most violent debates, which took place in the House of Lords, in February 1775, even Lord Mansfield, a man in high consideration, and of great talents, but whom the Whig Party considered as an exaggerated partisan of the crown's rights, and as one of the most decided enemies of the Americans, carried away by the heat of the contest, formally declared, that the introduction of imposts, in the year 1767, was the most *absurd* and most *pernicious* measure that could have been decided, and had been the real cause of all the subsequent misfortunes.

17 Most of the colonies were founded before the middle of the seventeenth century; all before the revolution of 1688. The province of Georgia, the most southern of the colonies, and which was originally part of South Carolina, was the only one, which received her *separate* constitution since the beginning of this century (in 1732) and was likewise the only one for the settlement and cultivation of which the British government had been at any cost.

18 This is undoubtedly the greatest failing that can be objected against mixed governments. Fortunately, however, it must be acknowledged, that the probability of such a dissolution is more remote in proportion as the constitution approaches nearer to perfection. For the more easily one of the constituted authorities can resist the other, by its appropriate weight, the less will be the necessity of appealing to arms. On the other hand, the more imperfect the balance is, the greater will be the danger of a civil war. In this lies properly the decided superiority of the British constitution, above all other complicated forms of government, that ever were, or probably ever

will be devised.

19 In many places, the public officers appointed to collect the Stamp Tax were hanged up, or beheaded; but all, only in *effigy*.

20 Shortly before, the congress are said to have resolved upon a declaration, by virtue of which, the colonies offered, "not only for the future, in time of war, to pay extraordinary contributions, but likewise, provided they were allowed a free trade, for an hundred years, to pay an annual sum, sufficient in that period to extinguish the whole British national debt," and to have been deterred from giving their last sanction to this declaration, only by the account of new hostile measures of the parliament. This highly remarkable fact I mention however only upon the authority of a single writer, a very severe antagonist of the ministry, though otherwise very well informed. Belsham's Memoirs of George III. Vol. 2. p. 166.

21 I believe that in the first section of this Essay, I have completely shown the lawfulness of the American Revolution upon legal principles; and yet, in that analysis, it will be found, that the sphere of unalienable rights of man, and the sovereignty of the people, and the like principles, are not once touched upon.

22 The general opinion, and the unanimous testimony of all the known writers upon American affairs, leave scarce room for a doubt of this fact, though for the honor of the Americans I would most willingly call it in question. His *Common Sense* is a pamphlet just as contemptible, almost throughout just as remote from sound human sense, as all the others by which, in later times, he has made himself a name. To appreciate the character and tendency of this work, which, perhaps, has never been judged as it deserves, and to obtain a full conviction that it was solely calculated to make an impression upon

the mass of the people, and especially upon certain religious sects very extensively spread in America, the reader has only to remark the spirit of the author's favorite arguments, which are all drawn from the *Old Testament*, and the absurd reasoning, with which he attacks, not the king of England, but monarchy in general, which he treats as an *ungodly* invention. If such a work could have produced the American revolution, it would have been best for reasonable men to concern themselves no longer with that event. But it was certainly at all times, by the wiser and better men, considered, endured, and perhaps encouraged, only as an instrument to gain over weaker minds to the common cause.

The difference between this writer and the great authorities of the American revolution, such as Dickenson, John Adams, Jay, Franklin, &c. will be still more apparent, if we remark a similar difference between the two parties in England, which accidentally concurring in the same object, but differing infinitely from each other in the choice of means and arguments, declared themselves there in favor of that revolution. Whoever compares, for example, the writings of Dr. Price (who not-withstanding his numerous errors, deserves not, however, to be put in the same class with Paine) with the speeches and writings of Burke during the American war, will sometimes be scarcely able to convince himself, that both were contending for one and the same thing. And, indeed, it was only nominally, and not substantially, one and the same thing, for which they argued.

Another indirect, but not unimportant, proof of the accuracy and necessity of the distinction here pointed out, lies in the unquestionable aversion of most of the great statesmen in America to the French revolution, and to all what since 1789, has been called revolutionary principles. A remarkable anecdote occurs, testified by a witness unobjectionable upon this point, by Brissot, a man afterwards but too famous; an anecdote which proves how early this aversion had taken place. In a conversation which, shortly before the breaking out of the French revolution, he had with Mr. John Adams, now President of the United States, this gentleman assured him he was firmly convinced, that France, by the approaching revolution, would not even attain the degree of political liberty enjoyed by England; and what is most important, he denied, in perfect consistency with his pure and rigorous principles, that the French had a *right* to affect such a revolution as they intended. Brissot attempted in vain by appeals to the *original compact*, to the imprescriptibility of the rights of the people, and the like revolutionary rant, to combat him.—P. Nouveau Voyage dans les Etats Unis de l'Amérique, par Brissot. Vol. I. p. 147.

23 I purposely say, there was nothing of *itself* illegal in this alliance. For France found the independence of the colonies already founded, when she contracted an alliance with them, and might besides not shrink from the question as to the lawfulness of this independence. Nothing of *itself*, unnatural, or self-destructive; for the principles of the Americans contained immediately nothing, which could in any manner be dangerous to the existence of the French monarchy: and the political and commercial interests of this monarchy seemed in a manner to force its taking a part in the American revolution.

All this however notwithstanding, I believe, with the most intimate conviction, that a more profound policy than that of the count de Vergennes, and a larger and more comprehensive view into futurity, would have prevented France from contracting that alliance. Not to mention the false calculation which burdened with a new debt of one thousand millions of livres, a state already very much disordered in its finances, in order to do its rival, in the most favorable contingency, an uncertain damage. The whole undertaking was resolved on without any real political regard to its remote consequences. The lawfulness of the American revolution, might be ever so clearly demonstrated to a man capable of judging of its origin, and of appreciating the grounds upon which it was supported; the time might come, when without regard to the particular situation of the colonies, the general indefinite principle of insurrection might be taken alone, from their revolution, and applied to justify the most dangerous crimes. The Americans might ever so cautiously keep within their rigorous limits; and neither maintain, nor care for the application of their principles to other states; at the first great commotion, those whom the French cabinet had sent into the republican school, might with the forms consecrated in America, put all the European governments to the ban, and declare lawful and even virtuous under *all circumstances*, what had been allowable only *under certain circumstances*. These possible consequences of the co-operation of France would not have escaped the penetration of a truly great statesman, and the world has paid dearly enough for their having been overlooked.

24   In no one point is the analogy between the conduct of the revolutionary leaders in America and in France, so striking as in this; yet it must not be forgotten, that the Americans failed partly from inexperience and partly from real necessity; whereas in France they knew very well what they were about, and opened and widened the precipice with design.

The history of the American assignats, is almost word for word, only upon a smaller scale, and not attended with circumstances of such shocking cruelty, as the history of the French ones. The sudden start from two millions to two hundred millions of dollars; the credulity with which the first assignats were received, the undeserved credit which they for a time enjoyed, their subsequent rapid fall, so that in the year 1777, they already stood with specie in the proportion of 1 to 3; in 1778, of 1 to 6; in 1779, of 1 to 28; in the beginning of 1780, of 1 to 60; fell immediately afterwards to that of 1 to 150, and finally would pass for nothing at all; the attempt to substitute a new emission of assignats, instead of those which were worn out, continued until at last it became necessary to establish a formal depreciation; the harsh laws made to support the value of the paper; the regulation of the price of provisions (the maximum) and the requisitions, which they occasioned; the general devastation of property, and disturbance of all civil intercourse; the wretchedness and immorality which ensued upon them—all this goes to compose a picture, which the French revolutionary leaders seem to have taken for a model. It is remarkable, that they closely copied the Americans only in two points, of which one was the idlest, and the other the most objectionable of any throughout their revolution; in the Declaration of the Rights of Man, and in paper money.

Printed in Great Britain
by Amazon